Merry Christmas to the

Kubiak family

Your beautiful

gardens home

would be the envy of

this holiday home in

Spain with its colorful

garden maybe you should

write a book complete with pictures

The Butsch's

with love

ABSENTEE GARDENER SPAIN

SUSAN PENDLETON

ANAYA PUBLISHERS LTD
LONDON

First published in Great Britain in 1989
by Anaya Publishers Ltd, 49 Neal Street, London WC2H 9PJ

Editor Angela Gair
Designer David Robinson
Illustrators Jan Davies, Val Hill and Jan Smith

British Library Cataloguing in Publication Data
A CIP catalogue record for this book is available from The British Library

ISBN 1-85470-001-4

Typeset by Central Southern Typesetters, Eastbourne
Colour origination by Marfil, S.L. (Madrid)
Printed in Spain by Novograph, S.A. (Madrid) D.L. M-23.296

Susan Pendleton would like to thank Sra. Leslie Lake, Sra. Felisa Loria,
Vicente, Mary Carpenter, Clive Innes, Margaret Ayrton, Raya Hanbury,
Marion McQuarrie

The publishers would like to thank Stanley Collins especially for his valuable
advice and for the loan of photographs from his collection.

PHOTOGRAPHIC ACKNOWLEDGEMENTS

Most of the photographs in the book were taken
by the author but, in addition, the publishers
would like to thank the following people for
allowing their photographs to be included:
Stanley Collins p48 (top), p49 (top) and p61 (top);
Derek Gould p51, p66 (bottom), p76 (both), p77,
pp78/9, p79, p81, p82, p84 and p85;
J. Allan Cash p53.

CONTENTS

INTRODUCTION

Several years ago, driven by the worst British summer on record, my husband and I decided the time had come to seek out a haven in the sun, a place where we could escape the rat race – and the rain – even if only three or four times a year. After much careful searching, and with the valued help and advice of friends, we finally settled on a 1,000 sq m plot on a hillside in Spain, overlooking the Mediterranean.

Initially we concentrated on building our house and furnishing it. We then took our first proper look at our land: a miniature moonscape of dereliction and abandoned building materials! I had over the years spent much time and effort in recreating and transforming neglected gardens in England: I had also assisted my daughter and son-in-law with the design and planting of their two-acre garden in Zimbabwe. But this was definitely the biggest challenge I had yet faced. Here I would be starting a garden absolutely from scratch, on unfamiliar soil and in a hot, dry climate.

We thought the best solution for our hillside garden would be to create a 'large rockery', dotted with trees and shrubs. This, of course, was not the solution. When it rains in Spain the water cascades down the hillsides in great torrents, carrying with it plants, soil, rocks and stones. We very soon realized why the Spanish, along with the inhabitants of most other Mediterranean countries, terrace their land by cultivating horizontal 'steps' out of the hillsides, so as to retain precious rainfall and enable the grower to have easy access to plants and crops. It became clear to us that we would have to carefully plan the landscaping of the garden and, little by little and as the bank balance would allow, have parts of it terraced.

Back in England, we managed to find some information on plants suitable for dry climates and Mediterranean gardens in general. Hardly a flying start, but it enabled us to draw up a basic plan of how to lay out our plot. Through a process of trial and error (mainly the latter!)

we gradually got to know which plants are best suited to the Spanish climate and that need the minimum amount of attention. However, had there been some advice available to us. we would have been saved a lot of effort and heartache in getting our garden established. The only gardening books we were able to find were relevant to permanent residents in Spain, but not to the many people like ourselves who want to create an attractive garden but who cannot be on hand all year round to nurture it.

If you are in a similar position, I hope this

book will help you to overcome the kind of problems that we experienced, as well as to avoid the mistakes that we made. It is written especially for the absentee villa or apartment owner who has little or no knowledge of gardening in a hot, sunny climate such as that of the Spanish *costas* and islands. Whether you own a villa with a large garden or an apartment with a balcony, whether you have a new garden to establish or an existing one to improve, you will find that gardening in Spain is easier than you might think, once you know the ropes. With a little imagination and a small financial outlay over the years, you will be able to improve the appearance and the value of your property by surrounding it with attractive plants.

The main thing to remember is that gardening in Spain is very different to the kind of gardening we are used to in northern Europe, and in some ways it is much simpler. The soil may look poor when compared to the dark, crumbly stuff we are familiar with, but a brief walk around any garden or municipal park in Spain will confirm that the soil is capable of supporting a huge variety of marvellous, exotic shrubs, trees and plants. Most Mediterranean

Below The bougainvillea at its best. The large exotic blooms are borne for a very long season.

plants don't need to be fussed over: they are very resilient and will survive drought, wind and poor soil. There is no need for back-breaking chores such as double-digging: you simply decide where you want to position a plant, dig a hole, and plant it. Your garden can be colourful throughout the year, and will grow and bloom at a much faster rate in the warm Spanish climate. And finally, joy of joys, the endless battle with weeds, pests and diseases which we are so resigned to in damp northern climes, is far less of a problem in Spain.

You will also find that flowering times in Spain are a little different to those further north; spring flowers may begin flowering in early February, depending on the previous winter's weather. The best months for summer flowers are May and June. The hottest month, August, which is often the peak flowering time in northern European countries, is the least colourful month in Spain: by then, the summer flowers have given of their best and died down.

Do not despair if on occasions your plants do not seem to be progressing – they will pick up again eventually. After our first season of planting, we arrived in Spain the following September thinking that our plants would have doubled in size and be in full bloom. What a shock we had! There had been very little rain the previous winter and the summer had been particularly hot and dry. Even though we had a gardener watering once a week during the summer months, our plants had shrivelled up and practically disappeared. After that holiday we returned to England somewhat dejectedly, thinking we had wasted our time trying to create a garden at all. However, when we returned to Spain the following Easter, we could scarcely believe how our garden had grown. This time there had been plenty of rain during the winter, and the plants had recovered miraculously, sprouting new branches and lush green foliage. We had arrived prepared to start all over again with our garden, but found that it was not necessary. The lesson we learned was that even though new plants may appear to fail during a period of drought, it is well worth leaving them alone for a season or two as they are more than likely to recover.

The Spanish people have a certain empathy with nature that is much to be admired. They accept the extremes of their climate with a quiet stoicism. The unrelenting summer sun, and the often violent storms that can destroy a season's crops overnight, are all part and parcel of gardening in Spain. You too will find that some years your plants will flourish, while in others they may not do so well: so much depends on how much rainfall there is in winter and on how dry and hot the summer is. On the other hand, if the seasons have been kind, as is usually the case, your garden will grow, bloom and multiply. Always remain optimistic and remember that every little effort is rewarded.

For the absentee gardener, choosing the right plants – ones that are drought-tolerant and that require little attention – is the secret of success. Planning a colour scheme for your garden is important, too. In Spain, brightly coloured flowers, climbers and shrubs look spectacular against a backdrop of azure sky and the dazzling white walls of the houses; nevertheless, it is easy to be beguiled by bright colours and to make mistakes. One example that comes to mind is that of a villa I once saw which had bright orange sunblinds at the windows – and a cerise bougainvillea climbing up the walls! The beauty both of the plant and of the house were spoilt by this clash of ill-chosen colours.

There are many excellent garden centres and markets in Spain that stock a wide range of plants and seeds, as well as offering help and advice. One word of warning, though: Spanish garden centres and markets are somewhat 'laid back' when it comes to plant names. Many have their own local names for plants, which vary from one area to another, and this can be confusing. When we first arrived in Spain, full of enthusiasm, and waved our 'shopping list' of plants, with their proper botanical names, in front of the local garden centre attendant, we were nonplussed to discover that he hadn't a clue what we were talking about. In writing

this book I have tried my best to find the most generally used Spanish equivalents for the plants I recommend, to spare you the embarrassment that we experienced, but it has not been easy! When you visit garden centres in Spain, it may save time and avoid confusion if you can take along with you photographs of the plants you wish to buy.

If you decide to take seeds, plants or bulbs with you to Spain, you will need to obtain a health certificate for them. If your base is in Great Britain this can be obtained from your local Plant Health Director who, for a small charge, will send samples of the seeds or plants you wish to take to the Plant Pathology Laboratory at Harpenden in Hertfordshire. If they are clear of disease, he will issue you with a PHYTO Sanitary Certificate which will enable you to take them through Customs on entry into Spain. More information can be obtained from the Ministry of Agriculture, Plant Health Division, Room 504B (LER), Nobel House, 17 Smith Square, London SW1P 3HX (tel: 01-238 6483).

Above *Our garden in spring. Three years ago this was just a bare rocky slope; now it is a lovely terraced area graced with colourful plants.*

Five years after we first started, our garden in Spain has grown and matured, and now more or less looks after itself. Friends have been more than complimentary, and it is they who have encouraged me to write this book to show how a beautiful garden, balcony or patio can be created by an amateur gardener, and with very little attention from one visit to the next. When we first started we made lots of mistakes and put plants in all the wrong places, but perfecting our garden each year has become part of the fun and enjoyment of visiting Spain, and is always something we look forward to when we go on holiday. Even if, like us, you can only visit your holiday home a few times during the year, you can have the pleasure of growing wonderful, colourful plants and flowers all the year round. Good luck, and happy gardening!

Susan Pendleton, April 1989

PLANNING
YOUR
GARDEN

1

THE WELL-PLANNED GARDEN

If you are faced with a completely new garden, attached to a house that has just been built and consisting of a bare patch of soil studded with builders' rubble, your first instinct might be to rush off to the nearest garden centre and buy armfuls of plants to cover up the bareness. There are some things in life, however, that can't be rushed, and planning a garden is definitely one of them. Decisions made in haste and on impulse are often regretted, and mistakes can be expensive and time-consuming to put right. A well-planned garden, on the other hand, is relatively easy to look after and will give you many years of pleasure.

Before planning the layout of the garden, make a list of the features you want to include in it. Do you intend building a swimming pool or patio? Might you want a lawn or a rock garden? Where will the garden paths be sited? Do you need to allocate an area where children can play?

Aspect and climate

Having made a checklist of practical and ornamental features you want to include, the next thing to consider is the aspect of your garden, because this will have a bearing on where you decide eventually to position, say, the patio, in order that it receives some shade.

Sun

Does your garden face north, south, east or west? Observe which areas receive the most sunlight and which are shaded. The sun is extremely powerful in southern Spain, so there is no point in putting shade- or moisture-loving plants in a corner of the garden that receives unremitting sun all day long during summer: instead, this is the area in which to plant succulents and other desert-type plants, which thrive in these conditions.

Pavements and walls that face south store the sun's heat during the day and radiate it at night; cold-sensitive plants such as bougain-villea may be grown against such a wall with great success, yet fail miserably just a few feet away in an open position. North-facing walls will be cooler and more shaded than those facing south, so shade-tolerant plants should be sited here.

Wind

The direction of the prevailing wind is another point to bear in mind. In summer the hot, dry wind known as the *Levante* often comes when least expected and can devastate a garden in an exposed situation (not to mention the drying effect it has on soil and plants). In winter the wind can be strong and cold, damaging green foliage and stunting the growth of shrubs and plants that aren't protected. If your garden is in an open situation, you can provide protection from the wind by planting a tall hedge or groups of conifers and hardy evergreen shrubs around the margins of the garden, to act as windbreaks.

Water

One very important point to consider is how much water you have available for watering the garden. In northern Europe we take for granted a constant and unlimited supply of water, but along the Spanish *costas* it is a much more scarce commodity. Some areas normally have adequate supplies, but in others, as you have probably discovered, supplies are sometimes rationed, particularly during the summer months. If water is limited in your area, your dreams of a beautiful, manicured lawn are likely to end in disappointment; think about a paved or gravelled area instead. Similarly, you will need to choose and site your plants carefully. It is a good idea to position close to the house those plants that need regular watering. The rest of the garden can be filled with plants that need little or no water. There are a surprising number of drought-resistant trees, shrubs and plants, which will shade, screen or

cover the ground just as efficiently as the water-demanding varieties.

Above It took us two years to transform a building site into a paved and terraced garden.

Financial outlay

Starting a garden from scratch, or even altering an existing one, can be an expensive business, so make sure you plan within your budget. If you are planning major projects such as a patio, pool or paved area, there will be a large initial outlay in building materials and labour costs. Those of you who are going to be away for much of the time may want to consider paying a gardener to water your plants, especially during the hot, dry months from late May through to October.

The cost of water will also feature in your calculations. In Spain the water supply is metered, so the more you use the more you pay, and water is not particularly cheap. Although this book recommends plants that survive on little water, they will nevertheless need some, particularly during the summer months, so bear in mind from the outset how much you are prepared to spend on your water bill.

If the soil in your garden is poor or dry you may have to buy quantities of topsoil, manure and compost, which again are not cheap. And all this before you've bought even a single plant!

After making careful plans and estimating the total cost of initial outlay and general upkeep, you may find you have to begin with fewer plants than originally envisaged. If this is so, plant trees and shrubs first: they take longer to grow, but they will eventually form the backbone of your garden. If you want instant colour you can fill the gaps with the ever-faithful geraniums, which can be bought cheaply at local markets and garden centres, and then gradually add larger shrubs as your bank balance allows. Weed growth in a hot climate is very slow, so with any luck your bare patches will stay bare until you can afford to fill them.

DESIGNING YOUR GARDEN

Drawing up a sketch plan of how you'd like your garden to look helps to formulate your ideas. Your aim is to find a way of fitting everything into a pleasing design, within the limitations imposed by climate, aspect and your existing budget, and it is better to have a broad but flexible idea of what you hope to achieve than to create a garden in piecemeal fashion.

Before deciding on your final design you will probably sketch several possible layouts, before coming up with a solution that is both attractive and workable. Trial and error on paper costs nothing, and will save you a lot of blood, sweat and tears – not to mention money – in the long term.

Making a plan

Make a sketch plan showing an overhead view of your existing garden, indicating the boundaries and any existing features such as trees, flower beds, paths, hedges and patios. Draw in the house walls that face onto the garden and mark the position of the windows.

Mark in any other relevant details, such as the direction of the prevailing wind, sunny and shady spots, north-facing walls and areas of poor soil.

Measure the dimensions of your plot and then draw up your sketch plan to scale on squared paper to give you an idea of proportions and relative distances between one area of the garden and another. If you take one graph square to equal one square foot or one square metre, it will then be easy to draw to scale.

Include on your plan those features that you want to keep or that cannot be moved. Then look at the remaining space and decide where you might want to position new features, plant trees, and so on. As you position each element, consider whether it is best in sun or shade; close to the house or well away; whether or not it needs shelter from the wind; and so on.

Making the plan work

Garden design, like the design of the interior of a house, is very much a matter of personal taste. There are no hard-and-fast rules, and ultimately you are the person who has to live with your garden and like it. That said, however, arranging the elements of a garden is not quite as easy as arranging furniture in a room, simply because in planning a garden you have to rely on your imagination to a much greater extent. A mature garden with terraces, a lawn, shrubs and trees cannot be achieved overnight: you have to lay the foundations now for what you *hope* your garden will look like in three or four years' time. This applies particularly if you are dealing with a brand-new garden; it's like being given a huge sheet of paper upon which you have to draw a well-composed picture – without the aid of an eraser!

Overleaf are a few brief guidelines to help you design a garden that will look pleasing and will reflect your taste and lifestyle:

1. Oleander
2. Schinus
3. Fan Palm
4. Olive Tree
5. Hibiscus
6. Datura
7. Myporem
8. Cotoneaster
9. Lavender
10. Jacaranda
11. Cestrum Nocturnum
12. Yucca
13. Canary Palm
14. Agave
15. Canna
16. Agapawthus
17. Zantedeschia
18. Carob Tree
19. Pine Tree
20. Geranium
21. Jasmine (White)
22. Mimosa
23. Carpobrutus/ Lampranthus
24. Chrysanthemum Frutescrews ("Margaritas")
25. Gazania
26. Pampas Grass
27. Lemon Tree
28. Orange Tree
29. Herb Garden
30. Dianthus
31. Solandra
32. Bougainvillea
33. Wisteria
34. Plumbago
35. Bignowia Rosa
36. Solanum Wenlandii
37. Thunbergia
38. Tecomaria Capensis
39. Cupressus Horizontalis
40. Pots of Geraniums, Dianthus, Lotus Berthelotii, Oleanders, Palms, Bay Trees etc.

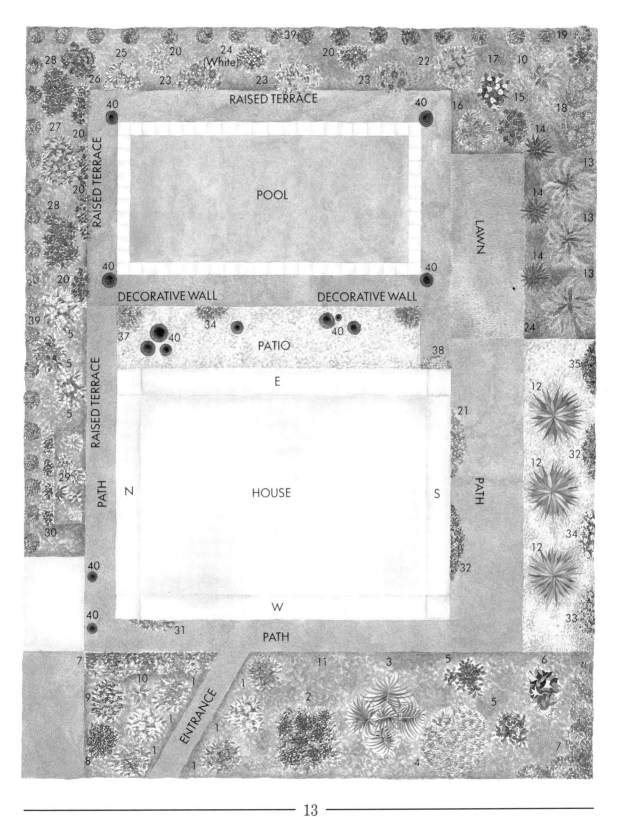

RAISED TERRACE

RAISED TERRACE

POOL

LAWN

DECORATIVE WALL   DECORATIVE WALL

PATIO

E

RAISED TERRACE

PATH

N

HOUSE

S

PATH

W

PATH

ENTRANCE

28
25   20   24
            (White)
39   20   22
26   17   10
    23   23   23   16   15   18
40   RAISED TERRACE   40   14
27
20   14
20   13
28   14
20   13
40   40
37   40   40
34   38
39   21   35
5   12
5   32
5   12
29   34
30   12
40   33
40
31
7
10   11   3   5   6
1   5
9   1   2   5
1   1   7
8   1   4

PLANNING YOUR GARDEN

● Keep it simple. Intricate layouts make a small garden look even smaller, and are difficult to maintain. Think of your plants in groups rather than in isolation.

● Restrict straight lines as much as possible. Gentle, sweeping curves are more sympathetic to a natural environment, and also make a small garden look larger.

● A garden should not reveal all of its attractions in one brief glance. To make a garden seem bigger and more exciting, create a few hidden corners that offer surprises and fresh new vistas as you walk through it. This can be done by erecting a hedge, a group of tall shrubs, a pergola or a trellis covered with climbers at right-angles to the side boundary, so that the view beyond is partially hidden.

Right *A gravel path, attractive climbers and decorative terracotta pots provide an inexpensive, low-maintenance way of dealing with an awkward space at the side of a house.*

Far right *The white stone steps provide a natural focal point in this garden.*

• Create a focal point or two – perhaps a statue, an arbour or a colourful specimen tree. By placing these at key points in the garden, you will lure the viewer's eye into the distance and thus create a strong impression of depth.

• Relieve the mainly horizontal planes of the garden by planting tall shrubs, trees and climbers, which add a vertical dimension.

• Balance colourful planting areas with visually restful ones, such as a lawn or a paved area.

Choosing plants

Before buying new plants for your garden, it makes sense to do some research into the plants that grow well in your local area and that are suited to the type of soil you have in your garden. Visit places such as local parks and botanical gardens, where you can see plants actually growing, to get an idea of their size and shape. Note which varieties have been chosen and grouped together, for you can be sure that these plants have been carefully selected because they are both pleasing to the eye and easy to maintain. Local garden centres will be able to offer advice on suitable varieties for your particular situation. Take a look, too, at your neighbours' gardens, to see what grows successfully and what does not.

In Chapter Three of this book you will find a comprehensive guide to trees, shrubs, plants and flowers that can successfully be grown in Spain, along with information on shape, height, colour and flowering period, and advice on positioning, light and water needs, and pruning.

Lawns

The decision to grow a lawn is one that needs careful consideration if you are an absentee gardener, for obvious reasons; a lawn needs frequent mowing, watering, feeding and weeding, and periods of drought may prevent the lawn from establishing itself in the first place. You may decide to opt instead for some more permanent kind of covering, such as tiles, paving or gravel, which are comparatively trouble-free. However, if you have made up your mind to have a lawn, tips for planting are covered on page 91.

SWIMMING POOLS

A swimming pool should ideally blend into your garden and can become a very attractive feature of your landscape. If your villa is newly-built and you are planning to build a pool, there are a number of points to consider before doing so. First of all, the size and shape of the pool need careful thought. Bear in mind that water is generally scarce, and that it can be expensive to buy enough water to fill a large pool. (You must also ensure that the water is constantly topped up to a level above the filter throughout the year so that the filter mechanism can work correctly.) A small pool may suit your requirements just as well as a large one, and is cheaper to filter and heat as well as requiring less water and chemicals.

It may be worth mentioning here – for those of you who have no experience of maintaining a pool – that it is advisable not to empty the pool at the end of the summer and then fill it again at the beginning of the following summer. Both frost and heat can crack exposed tiles. It is much more sensible to keep the pool filled all year round and hire a local pool maintenance firm or a gardener to look after it.

If you plan to do a lot of entertaining in the evenings, you may wish to consider installing lights around your pool. These can look very attractive, especially if positioned to reflect on to the water. You can even have lights installed underneath the water. If your pool hasn't yet been built, take the opportunity to plan the electrical wiring now, before the tiles have been laid and the pool has been filled.

Positioning the pool
The position of your pool needs careful planning. Is it to be a dominant feature, or would you prefer it screened off from your house behind a fence or hedge? Look for a sheltered position unexposed to wind and screened from the view of passers-by. If you have small children, you may want the pool to be easily visible from the house so that you can keep an eye on them. And finally, if your pool is not going to be heated, try to position it so that it receives the maximum amount of sunshine during the day.

Poolside plants
Foliage and plants around your pool will add colour and interest to the pool landscape, as well as creating a natural and decorative setting. Choose poolside plants carefully so that they blend in and form a link between the pool and the landscape beyond.

The area immediately around the pool will probably be tiled or paved. Tiles and paving stones absorb the intense heat of the sun and then in turn give off warmth during the night. Palms, agaves and cacti make suitable poolside plants, perhaps intermingled with attractive rocks and stones. These plants will survive

drought conditions and need no attention. If you have small children, be careful to keep cacti and agaves with large spikes away from the edges of paved areas.

Tall trees and shrubs will add style and elegance to the poolside area. Make sure they are evergreens though; deciduous trees can create a litter problem when they shed their leaves during the autumn. Take care not to plant trees with root systems that are attracted to water or drainage systems, as they can damage a pool's foundations: trees to avoid are figs, weeping willows and eucalyptus.

Shrubs and small trees can be planted near the edges of the pool; plant them in groups in varying sizes, rather than singly. This will keep the overall appearance simple and uncluttered. Alternatively, group smaller plants in raised beds which can be constructed from brick or natural stone.

You may prefer to have large decorative pots full of flowers strategically placed around your pool. A few pots containing large shrubs such as oleander, a bay tree or a palm look strikingly elegant, as do pots of trailing geraniums. Take care not to overcrowd the area: two or three large pots carefully placed have a much better effect than five or six smaller pots.

If you plan to have a lawn, it can be taken right up to the edges of the tiling, or you can leave a border along the edge of the tiling and plant shrubs such as hibiscus and oleander, or palms and yuccas interplanted with spring bulbs or clumps of agapanthus.

If you need to create a screen between the pool and the rest of the garden, you can choose from cupressus, oleander or myporem as a hedge. Or you may prefer an ornamental wall in stone or wrought iron in front of which you can plant scented climbers.

Left A simple planting scheme provides a natural link between the pool and the rest of the garden. One or two large terracotta pots provide accents around the pool margins.

PREPARATION AND PLANTING

2

PREPARING YOUR PLOT

A garden that has perfect soil is rare. This is particularly true of many gardens in southern Spain, where the harsh limestone soil appears dry and inhospitable. If your new garden plot looks more like a building site, just lumps of rock, stones, sand and dust, you will find it hard to believe at first that you can grow beautiful plants.

However, evolution has enabled plants to adapt themselves to extremes of soil type and climate, and by choosing those plants that are adapted to a dry habitat (many of which are recommended in the following chapter) you are assured of good results.

In addition, there are steps you can take to improve your soil and give your plants the best possible start. Although different plants have different cultural requirements, they all demand a good soil that drains well and contains the necessary nutrients, an adequate supply of sunshine and water, and protection from extremes of temperature.

We are all anxious to rush out to garden centres and buy masses of plants, but the

Below Here you can see how each individual plant has been mulched to prevent moisture loss from the roots as well as providing vital nutrients.

cultivation of the soil and the preparation of the plot should be completed first. The more fastidious you are in preparing your soil the better-lasting results you will achieve with your plants. If your soil is of poor quality, take a delivery of topsoil and farmyard manure – your local garden centre should be able to help you with this. Although both topsoil and manure can be expensive to buy, they are a good investment since they will greatly improve the quality of your soil. If you are on a limited budget, a bag of manure, potting compost and a handful of general fertilizer added to the planting hole when you plant individual shrubs, trees or flowers will be just as effective in the short term. Heavy clay soils will benefit from an addition of sharp sand or fine gravel, together with compost and manure. This will help to aerate the soil and improve drainage.

Watering

The most basic requirement for plant survival is water. Always try to water plants *before* the leaves wilt, and water plentifully: simply wetting the surface encourages plant roots to develop close to the surface, where they will dry out even more quickly.

The best times for watering are in the early morning and the evening, when plants take up plenty of water and store it for the day. Watering in the middle of the day is wasteful, as the water evaporates more quickly.

In Spain, sprinkler hoses are seldom used when watering gardens. There is little point in watering the entire surface of the soil, as the moisture evaporates so quickly in the heat. The most efficient method is simply to give each individual plant a thorough soaking with a hand-held hosepipe. It is a good idea to build a shallow ring of soil around each plant, to form a water-retaining 'basin'. Allow the basin to fill up with water before moving on to the next plant. This way, the roots of each individual plant will get the maximum amount of water.

In a hot, dry region such as southern Spain, water is a precious commodity, so when it is

Above *Careful preparation enables you to grow strong, healthy plants even in poor soil.*

available, use it wisely. During periods of drought, water supplies may be rationed in some areas and it may be necessary to collect water used in washing and cooking and use it to water your most valuable plants.

Mulching

Long periods of drought and hot winds in summer can leave the soil in your garden baked and dry, especially if water is rationed due to shortages. Spreading a layer of good compost or manure around the base of plants – a method known as mulching – will help to keep the soil moist by reducing water evaporation. The best time to apply a mulch is in spring, while the soil is still damp from winter rains.

TOOLS AND EQUIPMENT

There is such a wide range of garden tools available that it can sometimes be difficult to make a choice. Most gardeners rely on a basic set of tools and equipment for garden chores, and add to their armoury as the need arises. The main thing is to buy good-quality tools, as cheaper models are likely to be uncomfortable to use and less durable. The following tools may be regarded as essential for gardening in Spain.

Mattock

A mattock, or Spanish hoe, is invaluable for digging dry, stony ground and hard, sun-baked soil. It can be single-bladed or two-pronged.

Spade and fork

If you inherit a garden that has been well cultivated, you will find use for a spade, fork and hand trowel. Compare several before buying. A spade and fork should be well balanced and the weight and length of the shaft should feel comfortable.

Rake

A rake is useful for clearing rubbish, raking up stones and leaves and levelling gravel paths.

Secateurs

A strong pair of secateurs for pruning roses, trees, shrubs and climbers is most important. There are two main types: those with a scissor action and those that cut against an anvil. A good quality pair will last you well. Keep them clean and oiled. If you have large trees that need drastic pruning, you will also need a pruning saw and a pair of long-arm pruners.

Lawn mower

If you plan to have a lawn you will obviously need a lawn mower, whether hand-propelled or power-driven. There are three main types: cylinder mowers, which give the most professional results; rotary mowers, which don't give

1 Hose
2 Spade
3 Fork
4 Secateurs
5 Single-bladed
mattock or Spanish hoe
6 Two-pronged mattock

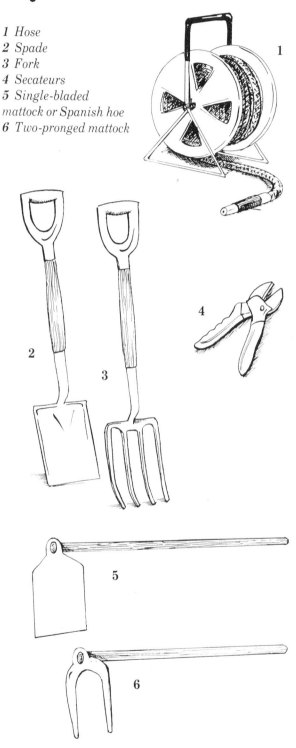

as smooth a finish, but are excellent for cutting long grass; and hover mowers, which work on the same principle as a rotary mower but are supported on a cushion of air, making them light and easy to handle, especially on sloping ground.

Hose

A general garden hose is necessary, and, if you have an unlimited supply of water, a sprinkler attachment is useful for watering lawns.

In addition to the above tools, you will need a shovel if there is gravel or topsoil to be spread; a watering can; a wheelbarrow; a hand sprayer for spraying insecticides; and a soft-headed broom (a hard-headed broom is of little use in sweeping dusty paths, patios and balconies). We also needed a pickaxe on parts of our garden plot, but you may be more fortunate!

Always be sure to look after your garden tools. Don't leave them lying around where they will be exposed to sun, wind and rain, or cause accidents. I know it's a chore after a hard day's work in the garden, but always clean tools before putting them away. Scrape off as much dirt as possible, then wipe the blade or prongs with an oily rag. It only takes a few minutes, and will prolong the life of your tools.

Right *If you have a neglected or unkempt garden to tackle, these are the basic tools you will need to begin with.*

PLANTING

Planting appears to be a simple operation, but if not carried out properly your plants will not grow strong and may even die. The more carefully the ground is prepared and the planting holes are dug, the faster the plant will be able to make new growth.

The best time for planting is from the end of October to January. However, for the absentee gardener, planting can be done from September up until the end of May provided you are able to water every day at first, and regularly throughout the first year.

There is a basic method of planting for *all* types of plant in this hot, dry climate, which is outlined below.

• Begin by marking out your plot. You may prefer to start with a small area and create your garden a little at a time. Perhaps you have a pine or carob tree, or some wild rosemary or thyme bushes already growing, and which might be in just the right position to provide shade or privacy. If you decide to keep them, clear the area around them of stones and debris. Add a dressing of topsoil or manure if necessary.

• It is most important that the planting hole is large enough to accommodate the roots comfortably so that they can spread out in search of moisture and nutrients. Dig the hole as deep as and slightly wider than the shrub's container or rootball. Check the hole for depth by inserting the plant: the old soil mark on the stem should be level with the surface of the surrounding soil.

• Fill the planting hole with water up to a level of 10–15cm (4–6in). This water should drain away within one or two hours; if the water remains after that time, dig the hole deeper. If the water still does not drain away, consider planting elsewhere, or alternatively choose plants which are suited to dry conditions, such as agaves, palms and yuccas. This situation occurs if you have a calcareous soil. This is a soil type which contains calcium carbonate, which is only slightly soluble in water. It often forms a thick layer of calcium, known as

1 Remove plant from container.

'caliche', beneath the surface of the soil. Plant roots find it impossible to penetrate this hard layer, and the plant may eventually die. If one area of your garden has this soil type, it does not necessarily mean that all of your garden is affected – other areas may have deeper soil.

• Break up the soil at the base of the hole and fork in some well-rotted manure or compost, then add a layer of soil – the rootball of the plant should not come in direct contact with manure. Prepare a soil planting mix of two parts soil to one part organic material, such as manure or compost. This fine, crumbly, moist planting medium will give the roots a good start.

• Carefully remove the plant from its container, *keeping the rootball intact*. This is most important; if you spread the roots they will quickly dry out. Remove any diseased or damaged top growth, cutting just above a bud. Set the plant in the hole and carefully press the soil mix around the roots to remove any pockets of air. When the hole is half full, gently firm the soil. Water in, then add more soil mix, firming again. The final soil level is important. Use the soil mark on the stem of the plant as a guide; it should be level with or fractionally under the surface of the soil.

• Trees and tall shrubs should be staked until they are established enough to support themselves. Insert the stake into the planting hole before planting, to avoid damaging the roots. Adjustable rubber straps should be used to attach the trunk to the stake and keep it in place.

• Water is crucial to a newly planted tree or shrub, for if the soil is allowed to dry out before the roots can take a hold the plant is likely to die. After planting, build a shallow ring of soil around the planting hole, about 30–45cm (12–18in) from the main stem, depending on the size of the plant, to form a water-retaining basin. This enables you to make a 'pond' of water around the plant, which soaks right down to the roots. The soil should be kept moist for at least a week or two, until the plant is established; the amount of water can gradually be reduced as the plant begins to grow.

• Apply a mulch of manure or compost around the base of the plant, to help retain moisture and cut down on watering. Applying a dressing of compost or general fertilizer in spring or autumn will give the plant a boost.

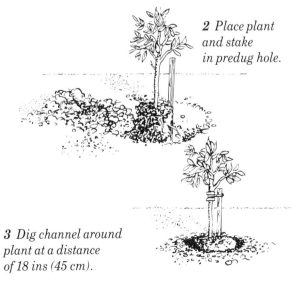

2 Place plant and stake in predug hole.

3 Dig channel around plant at a distance of 18 ins (45 cm).

Far left *Note that the planting hole is much larger than the rootball of the plumbago being planted.*
Above *Making a hollow around the plant enables water to get straight down to the roots instead of running off the surface of the soil.*

PLANTS FOR YOUR GARDEN

3

TREES

Even a small garden will benefit from the inclusion of a tree, or, if you have the space, a group of trees. The volume, colour and shape of ornamental trees will lend an air of maturity to your garden and give it stature. Trees can create shade, make a dull corner interesting, form an attractive backdrop for colourful shrubs and flowers, or be a central feature of your garden.

Trees take a long time to reach maturity, and for this reason you may be tempted not to bother with them. But even immature trees are highly attractive, and there is much pleasure to be had in returning to your villa each year and marvelling at the progress your trees have made.

Choosing trees

The number and variety of trees available is vast. When making a choice, consider why you are planting the tree and what its purpose is. Is it to provide shade or shelter? Or is it to be purely decorative? An ideal tree is one that gives pleasure throughout most of the year, bearing blossom in the spring, fresh foliage in the summer, and fruit and attractive colouring in the autumn. Evergreen trees, on the other hand, provide shelter from the wind and an all-year-round backdrop for your more colourful plants.

Siting

If you are starting a garden from scratch, it is generally advisable to choose your trees and site them before you plant your other shrubs and flowers. If you cannot afford to buy all your trees at once, concentrate on one area with a tree as the centre piece and build your garden from there, a little at a time.

Since a tree cannot be moved once it has reached maturity, great care must be taken about where to position it in the first place. As trees are expensive to buy, most of us have to buy them quite small, and it can be difficult to envisage the tree's eventual height and spread and how much shade it will cast. Shade can be welcome in a hot climate, but will it deprive nearby plants of light? Underground, there will be an extensive network of hungry and thirsty roots, so bear this in mind if you intend planting around your tree.

Avoid positioning trees too close to the house as the roots can damage drains and foundations. A large tree will take up a lot of water, and on clay soils this can even cause subsidence in a prolonged drought. If you have a swimming pool, remember that the leaves of deciduous trees will be a nuisance in autumn, so either choose evergreens or plant your tree well away from the pool. It may sound obvious, but it's amazing how easily these things can be overlooked!

Planting and aftercare

Since trees will become permanent residents in your garden, take care to plant them properly and nurture them until the roots are established.

When planting your tree, put plenty of organic material in the bottom of the planting hole. This will conserve moisture around the roots and provide plenty of nutrients. Trees need to be staked when young and tender: the wind is quite capable of breaking the top off a newly-planted specimen.

Knock in a stake about 15cm (6in) from where the trunk will be, *then* plant the tree – that way the stake won't damage the roots. Replace the soil and firm it, then tie the tree to the stake with two plastic ties. These hold the tree firmly away from the stake while at the same time giving it support. If you cannot obtain plastic ties, wrap a folded piece of cloth or a piece of rubber around the trunk, tie your string around this and then to the stake. Check the ties each year; as the trunk thickens they will need to be loosened, otherwise they can damage the bark.

Secure young trees to stakes with plastic ties, if available, or strong twine. Position the stake 15cm/6in from tree. Use two or three stakes to secure young trees in exposed areas.

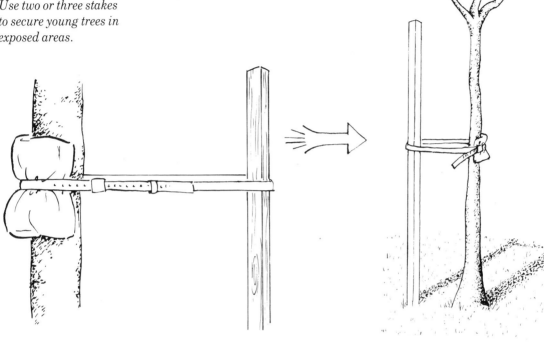

After planting, water in and apply a mulch around the base of the tree. If you give a tree good support, plenty of water until established, especially in the hot, dry months, a good dressing of compost and manure in the winter months, and a dressing of general fertiliser in spring, you will be richly rewarded.

Below is a brief survey of attractive, trouble-free trees for you to consider.

Citrus trees

It is always fun to grow fruit trees and to have the satisfaction of picking your own oranges or lemons while on holiday. Your local garden centre will be able to advise you on choosing the strongest and most resilient varieties.

Most of the citruses as well as bearing flowers and fruit are evergreen and therefore extremely useful for landscaping. Their glossy, deep-green leaves contrast with the bright yellows and oranges of the fruit and there is the fragrance of the blossom to be enjoyed, too. Plan for plenty of space around your trees; although they only grow to medium height they spread to a considerable width. Citrus trees thrive in a position that is open and sunny, but not in areas exposed to winds. If you have space only for one citrus, choose a lemon tree. The best time for planting citrus trees is from January to February. Once the fruits have formed, they take a further two to three months to ripen before they are ready to be picked.

Grapefruit

The grapefruit is one of the easiest citrus trees to grow. There are two kinds of grapefruit, one with pink, sweet-tasting flesh and the other with white flesh and a sharp, acid taste. Both types of fruit stay well on the tree and reach full maturity after a long hot summer. It is best to restrict the crop of fruit for the first two or three years until the trees are well established. They can grow up to 7m (23ft) in height and need little, if any, attention.

Lemon

Lemon trees are easy to grow. They need shelter from the winds and are very tender to frost, but don't require much water except weekly during the summer months. Prune hard in the winter months, shortening upright shoots by about one third and cutting out any crossed branches. The fruits are borne on the lateral branches.

Right and below *The ripening fruits of oranges and lemons add a welcome touch of colour to the garden in early spring.*

Orange

There are many different varieties of orange tree, and the fruits range from the bitter Seville orange used for making marmalade, to those that are known for their high juice content, and the sweeter oranges that are so good to eat picked straight from the tree. Different

varieties fruit at different times of the year. Often, trees are in blossom at the same time as the fruits are ripening.

Oranges are susceptible to diseases and pests such as aphids, and some people advise absentee gardeners not to grow them. It is worth experimenting with a strong, disease-free variety, which your garden centre should be able to recommend, but it is always advisable to spray against aphids at intervals throughout the year.

The Seville orange tree blossoms in spring, bears long-lasting, brightly-coloured fruit, is trouble-free and a vigorous grower.

Other fruit trees

Some other fruit-bearing trees that are suitable for growing in the ornamental garden include those listed below. Not only do they serve as attractive and colourful focal points, they also provide delicious and unusual fruits to eat.

Almond

For the absentee gardener the almond tree is an attractive choice, if only for its delightful delicate pink blossom in late January and early February. This can be picked when in bud and brought into the house to open. The tree should be sprayed against red spider mite and aphids when the flowers have set into fruits.

Almond trees need very little if any pruning, apart from cutting out any dead wood after the nuts have been gathered in August and early September.

Apricot

Apricots must be well watered during the hot, dry summer months. Choose a good variety

from your local garden centre and prune in the autumn, cutting out the centre branches to form a cup-shaped tree. A good feed of nitrogen when the tree begins to flower is advisable, and a spray with a preparatory insecticide after the fruit has set will help to keep the tree healthy and allow the fruit to form undamaged.

Avocado

The avocado is another tree suitable for this region, although it takes a few years before it produces a good crop of fruit. Plant in a position sheltered from the wind. If space is a problem there are dwarf varieties available. Prune mature avocado trees to restrict size and maintain productivity of the lower limbs by admitting light.

Left and above *The breathtaking beauty of almond trees in blossom in early February. The delicate pink flowers hang in clusters, often completely covering the tree, before the leaves appear.*

Fig

This is a large family of trees. You can grow the common fig for its fleshy edible fruit, or any one of the ornamental figs for landscaping. The tree grows to a considerable size and often the fruit causes a litter and insect problem in the garden. This tree should be planted only if you have a large garden: it needs to be kept well away from the house and pool as its roots can interfere with the foundations. It will produce a good crop of fruit if left alone. Prune occasionally during October or November to allow light into the centre of the tree.

Loquat

This is a very attractive, evergreen, medium-large fruit tree. The leaves are dark green and grow in a rosette pattern at the growing tips of the branches. The small, plum-shaped yellow fruits taste rather similar to a sharp lychee and are ready to harvest in late spring. The loquat is very popular in Spain and its popularity as an alternative fruit is spreading throughout Europe.

Pomegranate

This deciduous fruit tree is very easy to grow and can take any amount of wind, heat, drought and cold winters. It grows 2–3m (6–9ft) high and almost as wide. It has small, bright, glossy green leaves in summer, which turn golden before they are shed in the autumn. The flowers are bright red and the red-bronze fruit is filled with seeds surrounded by pulp which is sweet to eat. It is best pruned during late winter. The pomegranate is a very useful tree but it is important to remember that it is bare during winter.

Trees for landscaping

You may be fortunate enough to own a large garden that contains some of the taller, indigenous varieties of tree. These provide dramatic focal points in a garden, and require very little maintenance. Most landscape trees need only occasional pruning to improve shape, check height and spread, or to remove dead or diseased branches. Ideally the months from November to January are the best times to shape your trees, but if you are not at your holiday home during the winter months you can prune from October up until the beginning of April.

Acacia *(Mimosa)*

There are many varieties of acacia, more commonly known as mimosa, and they can often be found growing wild on roadsides and waste ground. *Acacia dealbata,* with its fine green feathery leaves, is a welcome sight in late winter and early spring, producing a mass of tiny fluffy yellow flowers. *Acacia rhetinoides* flowers during the summer months. Acacias are hardy trees, grow rapidly and love the sun.

Far left *The attractive, wavy-edged leaves and ripening fruit of the fig.*
Below *The lovely mimosa creates a magnificent show of colour in February.*

Carob

Another tree commonly found growing wild, and which you may also find in your garden, is the majestic carob tree which is native to parts of the Mediterranean, the Middle East and the warm southern regions of the United States. It is an evergreen, wide-spreading tree with rich green, crinkled, leathery leaflets and a heavily gnarled trunk. It bears long, fleshy pods that start out green and turn black as they ripen, and in which are enclosed the seeds or beans. The beans can be eaten and are used as a substitute for chocolate. Like the pine tree, if planted in the right position it can create shade and provide a very good backdrop for shrubs and flowers. It can take any amount of heat and drought.

Cupressus

Cupressus sempervirens (an upright tree as opposed to the *Cupressus horizontalis* suitable for hedging) is an excellent tree for your garden. It is a rich green conifer and grows very tall. It is particularly attractive grown at each side of an entrance or as a central feature surrounded by shrubs such as agaves or cacti. There are many varieties of cupressus, some with bright green leaves, others with silver

Above *The carob tree needs no attention and will provide welcome shade in any garden.*
Right *There is little to compare with the superb lilac-blue flowers of the jacaranda tree.*

grey or golden leaves. They are hardy and suffer extremes of weather, but take care not to leave them without water during a particularly hot, dry summer.

Eucalyptus

There are many species of eucalyptus tree, one of the most popular being *Eucalyptus polyanthemos* (Silver Dollar Tree). This tree is medium-sized and of moderately fast growth, with round grey-green leaves which can be dried and used for indoor arrangements. All varieties are attractive and fast-growing. They can be planted individually as specimen trees or in a row to provide a screen for privacy. Take care not to plant the eucalyptus near a pool, a drainage system or a well-watered area such as a lawn, as the roots will grow towards water and can cause structural damage.

Above *The attractive, blue-grey leaves of the eucalyptus have a pungent smell characteristic of the oil extracted from them.*

Jacaranda

For those of you who have visited Australia, Africa or South America, the tree that you probably most remember is the jacaranda. Long avenues of beautiful majestic trees bedecked with clusters of lavender-blue flowers line many roads in the cities. They are quite breathtaking and can grow many feet tall. The flowers are pendulous and the leaves fern-like. This is a beautiful tree to grow in your Spanish garden, particularly if it is surrounded by evergreen shrubs such as oleanders or hibiscus. It revels in heat and strong sunshine. It is deciduous and the leaves, flower petals and long seed pods all drop to the ground in the autumn. Prune from time to time to produce the desired shape. The jacaranda can also be trained into a large shrub.

Olive

If there is room in your garden for the venerable olive tree, what better tree to plant? Olive trees live for many years, enduring heat, drought and poor soil. The silvery leaves and gnarled trunk make an attractive feature in any garden. Although slow to grow at first, it becomes very large when fully matured. It tolerates desert conditions and apart from the times during the year when flowers and fruit are shed, which can cause a litter problem, they are very easy and trouble-free trees to grow. Not to be recommended for hay fever sufferers, though!

Canary Island Palm

This tree is a great favourite in Mediterranean gardens, and beautiful tall specimens can be found lining avenues and boulevards throughout the region. This will probably be your first choice of tree for your garden and the dry limestone soil found in many areas suits its cultivation exceptionally well. If you have a good-sized garden, try to buy the largest specimen

you can afford as they take many years to grow to full size. As your tree grows, carefully remove the lower fronds to form the trunk until the desired height is reached.

Pine

You may find that your garden has very little in it to start with apart from the common pine tree, which is perhaps a little straggly but with careful pruning may be worth keeping, particularly for the welcome shade it can give. Very little will grow underneath pine trees, but shrubs and other trees can be grown at a reasonable distance around them with very good effect. They need no attention at all except for hard pruning if their growth begins to encroach upon the surrounding plants.

Left Fan palms are strictly-speaking shrubs, but they grow to a considerable size.
Far left The noble olive tree, so much a part of the Mediterranean landscape.
Below Removal of the lower fronds of a Canary Island Palm will encourage trunk growth.

Schinus

The schinus, or pepper tree, is very beautiful and, like the pine and carob, tolerates both heat and drought. It grows like a weeping willow, very large and pendulous with fine lance-shaped feathery leaves. Small yellow flowers on the female tree produce clusters of red berries in summer and autumn. This tree grows up to 10m (33ft) high and very wide, so you will need to keep this in mind before planting. In the right position, particularly as it catches the wind, it can be a most attractive feature.

Tamarisk

This tree can be grown very successfully in arid regions and thrives near the sea. It tolerates intense heat, hot winds, drought and poor soil and is a vigorous grower. It will grow to about 10m (33ft) but can be pruned to any desired height and width. It has spreading branches covered with grey-green or light green, feathery foliage and tiny pink or creamy coloured flowers. It is ideal for a position where nothing else will grow and creates shade and an attractive grey-blue backdrop.

Above *The handsome schinus, or 'pepper tree', provides much-needed summer shade. Note the attractive antique pot in the background; you will find a huge variety of these in Spain.*
Right *A simple yet imposing entrance. The owner of the garden has made full use of the indigenous pine trees planted either side of a stone path.*

HEDGING PLANTS

A hedge can either form the outer boundary of your garden, giving privacy and acting as a valuable windbreak, or it can be used as an ornamental screen between different sections of the garden, around the pool, or to hide an unsightly feature such as a water storage tank or shed.

There is a wide variety of hedging plants which will grow quickly and form a very effective screen, but choose wisely if you need to cut down on maintenance as much as possible. Slow-growing evergreens, for example, require little maintenance pruning, whereas fast-growing shrubs require frequent clipping when used as formal hedges.

Hedges don't have to be tightly-clipped and formal; they can be allowed to assume a natural shape, with long, arching stems that carry flowers, fruits and decorative leaves – much more attractive to look at than the boring old privet we so often see back home! Informal hedges need only occasional pruning to restrict size and keep a pleasing shape.

When clipping a hedge, it is a good idea to shape the upper part narrower than the lower part, otherwise the top soon overgrows the bottom, depriving it of sunlight.

Most hedging plants can also be grown individually as shrubs, and these I describe in more detail later in the chapter.

Hedges for screening

Boundary hedges and hedges for screening need to be strong, of dense, bushy habit, and capable of growing up to a fair height.

Cupressus
Cupressus make excellent hedging plants and are often used to form windbreaks and shelter belts. They are tolerant of most soil conditions and provide a dense evergreen screen that is easy to care for.

There are about 20 different species of cupressus in the Mediterranean, but the most common type used for hedging is *Cupressus horizontalis*. Space the plants 30–35cm (12–14in) apart, either as a hedge or in a group or a row to make a windbreak. When the hedge has reached the desired height, it can be cut straight across the top, which allows the plants to fill out widthways and create a thick screen.

Below A tall cupressus hedge provides an impressive backdrop for mesembryanthemums tumbling over a low wall in the foreground.

During the spring and autumn, trim the sides to encourage thick new growth. Cupressus need more watering during their first year (and also in drought conditions) than does myporem, and they take longer to grow. They are also more expensive to buy initially, but they will produce a thicker, more permanent hedge in the longer term.

Myporem

A fast-growing hedge that is very cheap to buy is myporem, or what our Spanish gardener calls 'gandula' ('good for nothing'). This is an evergreen hedge with shiny green leaves which you also often see growing wild along-side motorways and river banks. It needs very little attention and will reward you with quick growth that forms a thick green screen. Plant the shrubs about 30cm (12in) apart, and when the hedge has reached the desired height and width, keep it closely clipped to ensure a thick, bushy appearance. If it becomes straggly and untidy after a particularly hot, dry summer, prune hard during the autumn or early spring to encourage strong new shoots to form.

Above *An oleander hedge with an abundance of pink flowers graces an attractive stone wall.*
Below *The lush, evergreen leaves of myporem – fast-growing, low-maintenance hedging plants.*

Flowering hedges

Many flowering shrubs make colourful and decorative hedges that are easy to maintain, requiring little more than a light clipping when the flowers have faded.

Oleander

The oleander is an evergreen shrub of Mediterranean origin and makes an extremely attractive hedge, especially along a low wall or against a wire fence. Planted about 60cm (24in) apart, the shrubs will thicken out and grow vigorously, producing a hedge up to about 2m (7ft) high within three to four years, with the added bonus of beautiful flowers that bloom from June right through to September or October. Some oleanders are sweetly scented and can be single or double, ranging in colour from white, pink, salmon and red to pale yellow. The blooms are offset by long, pointed, dark green leaves, although some varieties have leaves of variegated cream and green.

Once established, an oleander hedge is very easily maintained and has a lifespan of many years. Oleanders enjoy full sun and benefit from generous watering during spring, but will

crossed branches. A good spray with a preparatory insecticide during the spring and early summer is necessary as aphids may attack the new shoots and flower buds.

Low-growing hedges

Smaller and less robust shrubs can make attractive hedges within the garden, whether used as dividers or purely as an ornamental feature. Certain herbs, for example, can be grown as hedges that release a wonderful scent as you brush past them.

Lavender
The grey-green foliage of lavender can make a very attractive low hedge. Lavender can tolerate full sun and semi-drought conditions and produces strongly-scented blue flowers on long stems which can be picked for drying. Prune after flowering to keep bushes tidy.

Rosemary
This herb can be used as a medium-sized hedging plant in a particularly dry, sandy part of the garden. With its deep-green, aromatic leaves borne on woody branches producing tiny blue flowers in the spring, it also makes an effective backdrop for the low, brightly-coloured flowers you may choose to plant in your garden, such as geraniums, cannas and gazanias. Once established, a rosemary hedge will survive without watering and needs no attention apart from a trim and tidy once a year. To encourage strong growth and a bushy appearance, pinch out the tips of young shoots from time to time. The only drawback of a rosemary hedge is that after four or five years it can lose its leaves at the base and become untidy.

survive without. The flower heads should be cut off when dead to stimulate new shoots. If the plants have become straggly and untidy, cut back hard in October or November. Note that all parts of this plant are poisonous if eaten. They can be susceptible to greenfly but these can be cleared with a regular spray of a branded insecticide during March and April and again during June and July.

Oleanders are very versatile and can be trained into trees as well as hedges and bushes.

Hibiscus
The more common, hardy, red-flowering variety can be grown very successfully as a hedging plant. Position along a south-facing boundary sheltered from strong winds. The exotic, brilliantly coloured flowers are 7–10cm (2–4in) across and have a long yellow central stalk. The blooms last only one or two days but are produced continuously throughout the summer months. The best months for pruning are January and February. Shorten stems by about one third and cut out any dead wood or

These common, easy-to-grow hedging plants are only a few suggestions. There are many other shrubs which are suitable for hedging, such as *Tecomaria capensis* and pyracantha. If you have a gardener or a neighbour who can water your plants regularly, you can afford to be more adventurous in your choice of plants.

SHRUBS

Shrubs are the key to a garden that looks good all the year round. They provide shape, texture and colour, and give a mature, established look to a garden. They are particularly valuable between autumn and early spring: when the brightly coloured summer flowers have died down, shrubs keep the show going with their attractive berries and bark, unusual leaf colouring, fragrant flowers, and, in the case of evergreens, their foliage.

Shrubs are also extremely versatile. They can be used as boundary hedging or screening, hiding unsightly objects and giving a pleasant sense of enclosure; they will act as windbreaks, or provide shelter and shade for tender or shade-loving plants; they will hide or soften the straight edges of walls, driveways and paths; there are low-growing shrubs that form an effective ground cover that smothers weeds and prevents moisture-loss from the soil; there are tall shrubs that catch the eye and form a focal point at the end of a vista or path; and all form an effective background against which other plants may be displayed at their best.

Choosing and siting shrubs

Shrubs are long-lived and prefer to stay in one position, so it is important to choose and site them carefully. Some shrubs like full sun, others prefer light shade; some thrive on acid soils, others prefer alkaline soils. When stocking your garden, aim for a balanced mixture of evergreen and deciduous shrubs. Too many evergreens can look sombre and monotonous; too many deciduous shrubs will leave the garden looking bare in winter.

When planting out, bear in mind the eventual height and spread of the plants when they are mature and leave plenty of space between them. The space between two shrubs should be at least half the sum of their ultimate spreads. Shrubs that are overcrowded will be starved of nutrients, resulting in weak growth and poor flowering. Of course, spacing your shrubs correctly will leave gaps of bare earth, but remember that in Spain the growth rate of plants is much faster than in northern Europe, so you can be confident that the spaces will fill up within a year or two. Alternatively, you can use infillings of flowering perennials.

Planting

Since shrubs are a permanent feature it is important to plant them correctly. Container-grown shrubs can be planted at any time, except during the summer months, when the ground is baked hard and your supply of water may be limited. Bare-rooted shrubs can be planted from late autumn to early spring. To ensure good drainage and an adequate supply of nutrients, fill the planting hole with a mixture of topsoil and compost. After planting, water regularly to keep the soil moist until the plant is established: newly-planted shrubs will die if their soil dries out. A final dressing of compost and general fertilizer will help preserve moisture. For more detailed instructions on planting shrubs and trees, see pages 24–25.

Most shrubs, once established, need very little attention apart from a rejuvenating weekly watering in summer and a light pruning in winter to cut out dead wood and encourage strong growth in the following season.

The following are just a few of the many attractive shrubs you can grow in your garden in Spain. I have chosen those shrubs that are easiest for the absentee gardener to maintain, but you will no doubt be tempted by many others in your local market or garden centre.

Agave

This is a group of succulent plants noted for their attractive, fleshy leaves. There are many varieties to choose from, with leaves that vary in shape, size and colour. Your local garden centre will have a large selection on display.

Agaves are invaluable plants for the absentee gardener, as they thrive in poor soil and in

Above *Aeonium and agaves, two plants that are excellent for hot, dry areas of your garden.*
Right *Agave attenuata, which grows an unusual long, curved flower spike from its centre.*

extremes of heat, cold, sun and drought. They can grow extremely large, so be sure to plant them in a site where they will have sufficient space to grow to maturity. Because they often have sharp-tipped leaves, it is advisable to plant them well away from paths and areas that are in constant use. Ideally they suit large terraces and can be interplanted with a variety of other shrubs.

Agaves take several years to flower – seven or eight years at least – and once they have flowered they usually die. Over the years they will throw up many side suckers, which will in turn grow into mature plants.

Aloe

These are hardy, succulent plants, very similar in appearance to agaves. There are many different varieties, the most common being the *Aloe arborescens*. The leaves are fleshy and spike-tipped, but smaller than those of the agave, and form clusters of rosettes. They can grow into clumps up to 2m (6ft) wide if they are not divided. They produce long-stemmed spikes bearing red-orange flowers from late September through to November. They require much the same conditions as agaves and are a must for the absentee gardener.

Bamboo

Ornamental bamboo are tall perennial grasses of great value in the garden. With their airy, elegant shapes, they can create mood and character when planted among evergreen trees and shrubs. Their leaves are bright green, which in a sunny climate can give a refreshingly tropical look to your garden. Bamboo are at their best in areas sheltered from wind and strong sunlight. They will reward you if watered heavily from time to time and fed with a branded fertilizer to preserve the lush green appearance of the foliage.

Cestrum Nocturnum

This is an attractive shrub with long, thin, shiny, bright green leaves and pale creamy-white tubular flowers. The flowers are formed at the tips of the branches and open out at night, giving off a wonderful scent that fills the warm night air. The local Spanish name for this shrub is 'Galén de Noche'.

Cestrum Nocturnum is an easy shrub to grow, and produces suckers which can be removed with some roots attached and planted. It is susceptible to greenfly, which can cause the leaves to curl up. Spray with a suitable insecticide in spring and at intervals throughout the summer, making sure to spray the undersides of the leaves. Prune well during the autumn, cutting back some of the older branches completely and shortening young branches after the flowers have faded.

Cortaderia *(Pampas grass)*

These are hardy perennial grasses with ornamental foliage and large, feathery flower plumes which can be white, pink or lavender in colour, depending on the variety.

Cortaderia can spread into a very large clump up to 2m (6ft) wide. The flower plumes grow 1–2m (3–6ft) high in late summer, and the plant makes a very striking effect in sheltered areas or on lawns. The flowers last for many months and can be gathered for use in indoor

flower arrangements.

In order to keep these grasses lush and tidy, cut back after the flowering season, around December to January, to about 30cm (12in) off the ground. Feed and water as much as possible until new growth appears.

Cotoneaster

This genus contains a large variety of hardy evergreen shrubs bearing dark green leaves and brilliant red berries in November and December. They are suitable for open or shady positions and are easy to grow. There is no need to prune at all except for cutting back any dead wood and tidying into a desired shape.

Below *Pampas grass is an excellent plant to grow for wind protection. It produces elegant spikes topped with tall, feathery plumes in shades of cream or pink at the end of summer.*

Right and below The
datura is a magnificent
shrub, covered in large
trumpet-shaped flowers
which are very fragrant.
Some varieties have
double flowers.
Far right Hibiscus will
flower throughout the
summer, each flower
generally lasting for no
more than one or two
days. The large blooms
can be single, double or
semi-double, and are
very showy with their
long protruding central
stalk and flared petals.

Datura *(Trumpet flower)*

There are many species of this spectacular
shrub, but the most common in southern Spain
are those that produce fragrant white or
orange-red trumpet-shaped flowers, which
grow in great profusion from early to late
summer.

Datura grow to a large size and thrive best
in shade or semi-shade, in a position sheltered
from the wind. If you are able to water well
during the summer months, adding a little
fertilizer to the water every two or three
weeks, this shrub will reward you with a mag-

nificent show of blooms. Spray with a general insecticide in spring and early summer, and sprinkle pellets around the base of the shrub to deter snails. In February or March cut branches back hard to two or three buds.

The flowers and leaves are poisonous if eaten, therefore take care if you have inquisitive children!

Hibiscus

Hibiscus is a beautiful tropical shrub that grows up to 3m (10ft) high and produces large, showy, trumpet-shaped single or double flowers in many brilliant colours, including red, white, yellow and a range of oranges and pinks. It flowers continuously from late spring through to late summer (though each individual flower tends to last only one or two days) and can be used as a specimen shrub or mixed with other plants.

This shrub grows very easily but can be

affected by frosts and cold winds, so a sheltered position is preferable to one that is too open. If placed in direct sunlight it will flower profusely, but it must be watered regularly in a dry season.

Prune well after flowering, removing one third of the old wood each spring to keep the shrub bushy and encourage new growth. Spray against aphids in spring and early summer.

There is another species of hibiscus, known in Spain as 'Rosa de Siria'. It is deciduous and has smaller leaves and flowers than the standard hibiscus. The semi-double or double

Below *A sizzling colour scheme is created by the orange-red flowers of lantana combined with the pale blue flowers of plumbago cascading over a rocky wall.*

flowers appear in late summer and early autumn: they are produced in great quantities and in a wide range of colours, including blue, which is often a useful colour to have as it produces a cooling effect in the garden during the hot summer months. This species is more suitable for cooler gardens or shady areas. It is also frost-resistant.

Lantana

This shrub is extremely hardy, thriving in poor soil, extreme heat and constant sun, and produces flowers all year round in red, yellow, blue, purple and pink. *Lantana camara*, the species most commonly grown, can make a bush up to 3m (10ft) high and can be grown as a climber. Prune well in spring and remove any dead wood.

Lavender

Lavender is a familiar and well-loved plant, which has been grown for centuries. A dwarf perennial shrub growing 30–90cm (1–3ft) high, it has long-stemmed, fragrant flowers of white, pale lavender or purple, and blue-grey, lance-shaped leaves. The flowers have a delightful fragrance, and can be picked and dried for use in herb cushions and pot-pourris.

Lavandula pinnata flowers continuously, and with its hazy blue flowers and soft grey leaves it blends well with any colour scheme. It is also most effective when planted in rows each side of a path or an entrance, or around the base of a shaped orange tree.

Oleander

This is a dense, evergreen shrub that produces a mass of single or double flowers from mid-

Above *The flowers of lavender are highly aromatic. Here blue and white varieties are interplanted.*

summer until late autumn, many being sweet-scented. The flowers are very striking, with wide, flared mouths, and appear in a range of colours including white, cream, pink, salmon and crimson. The long, pointed leaves are also attractive, often being variegated in cream and green.

Oleanders were originally cultivated in the Mediterranean region and are particularly suited to hot, dry conditions. They will tolerate long spells of drought, but will produce the best flowers if watered well from time to time during the summer months and given a feed once a month. Spray the tips and the undersides of the leaves during early spring and summer to protect against aphids.

Above Oleander is a splendid long-flowering shrub for the absentee gardener.

This shrub grows up to 4m (13ft) high and to a considerable width. In a large garden three or four oleanders planted in a group will help to fill an open area very quickly and produce a wonderful splash of colour in the summer months. Planted in between palm or pine trees, the variegated-leaf variety creates a bold contrast. Take care to plant oleanders at least 60cm (2ft) apart to allow for growth.

Older plants can be rejuvenated by cutting three or four of the tough woody stems to the ground each year. If you plan to grow your oleander as a tree, prune to one or two stems and support with a stake until the stems thicken. Pinch off the lead shoots to encourage the stem to produce new leaves and flower buds. Oleanders also make suitable subjects for containers.

Palm
Although palms are mainly grown as trees, there are many varieties that can be grown as shrubs. The exotic foliage lends itself to many areas of the garden, and palms look particularly striking grouped around the margins of a swimming pool. Palms require very little water and will thrive in drought conditions. Your local garden centre will have a great many varieties for you to choose from.

Poinsettia
Poinsettia is the most famous species of the genus known as Euphorbia. It is characterised by the striking scarlet-red bracts that surround the tiny yellow non-descript flowers; you will be familiar with it as a house plant that is particularly popular at Christmas time. In Spain, along with other countries of a similar climate, it can be grown outdoors as a shrub.

This handsome shrub grows up to 2m (6ft) in

height. The red 'flowers' are at their best in November and December.

Prune after flowering, but take care to wash your hands thoroughly afterwards as the white sap that oozes from the stems is extremely poisonous and can cause irritation to sensitive skins. Cut back hard in April to produce a thick bush and plenty of flowers for the following Christmas.

Spanish broom

This is a bushy shrub, reaching up to 2m (7ft) in height and covered with sweetly scented blossom. The flowers take the form of typical, pea-like, broom flowers, and come in a range of colours, including white, pink, yellow and

Below Poinsettias appreciate well-drained soil and plenty of sun.

Right A splendid yucca underplanted with mesembryanthemums. Neither plant needs regular watering.

crimson. There are also two-toned varieties, in cream and yellow, yellow and crimson and pink and cream.

This is an excellent shrub for coastal regions as it will withstand wind and salt. It suits a dry, sandy soil and needs very little water.

Prune hard as soon as flowering is over, cutting back two-thirds of the previous year's growth. Unless you wish to reduce the size of the shrub considerably, never cut back into old wood.

Yucca

There are many species of yucca, the true desert plant, and all of them are very impressive to look at. The large flowering stem is covered with huge, creamy-white bell-like flowers hanging above an erect forest of spiky, lush green leaves.

Yuccas are happy in any sort of soil, as long as it is free-draining. They must have full sun. A yucca makes an eye-catching focal point, either as a specimen plant or as a vertical accent in a border. If you have a large garden they can be planted in groups, and the taller varieties can be grown as trees. No pruning is necessary except to trim away the dead flower stems and leaves.

CLIMBING PLANTS

No garden in Spain can be complete without its climbers. The dazzling white walls of the houses make a perfect backdrop for the brilliant colours of bougainvilleas, bignonias and a host of other splendid climbers that grow profusely in the hot Spanish sun.

If you've just moved in to a newly-built villa and the walls look a bit stark and bare, don't worry: a few climbing plants will soon clothe their nakedness and your home will blend more sympathetically with its surroundings. Climbers are particularly valuable since, once established, they provide such a spectacular display of colour in return for relatively little maintenance. Apart from the walls of the house, they can also be trained over fences, pergolas, garden sheds and even up old trees, providing another, vertical dimension to your garden.

Because of the hot, dry climate, a few practical steps need to be taken before planting. Climbers will need protection from the strong winds of both summer and winter, and they will need adequate sunlight and water. As mentioned earlier, evergreen trees and shrubs can be planted at angles to the house so as to reduce wind turbulence and create shelter for climbers and other plants.

When planting climbers against a wall, you will need to check that there is an adequate depth of soil for the roots to penetrate. Often the foundations of the building reach quite a way out. If this is the case, it is just not worth planting a climber, because the roots will have

Below *A car port is transformed by this lovely bignonia rosa scrambling over it. In front of it is a plumbago grown in a large pot.*

nowhere to grow and the plant will eventually die. In these circumstances it is often better to plant your climber in a large, deep pot; most of the climbing plants in Spain will thrive quite happily in these conditions.

Some climbers are self-supporting. Others will need tying in to a support, such as a wooden trellis or plastic netting, as they grow.

As a general rule, climbers need to be watered well until they are established and during the summer months. During November and December any hard old wood should be cut back by about one third. A good dressing of manure at this time, and a dressing of general fertilizer in the spring, will ensure a wonderful show of colour throughout the year. Spray with insecticide before and after flowering to guard against attack by aphids.

Bougainvillea

This is an extremely colourful climber, which can also be grown as a bush or a tree (with support) or trained to cascade over a terrace. The flowers are borne for a very long season, and often completely overpower the foliage.

The colours are brilliant – sharp pinks, bright reds, pale yellows, whites and oranges – and come not from the petals but from the leafy bracts that surround the flower.

Bougainvilleas are very easy to grow in Spain and are often at their most spectacular in hot, dry weather. The best position is against a south- or south-west-facing wall which is sheltered from strong winds. When planting from a pot, take care not to disturb the roots or the soil around them in any way. Water generously at first.

Once established, bougainvilleas need very little attention. January is the best time for pruning. The general rule is to prune back no more than 50cm (20in) of the leader shoots. This will encourage more side shoots to be produced. To ensure large clusters of coloured bracts to form tight against a wall, prune hard back when flowering is over.

Below Bougainvilleas grow prolifically in Spain. The white bracts of this variety look highly effective when contrasted with other, brightly coloured flowers.

Bignonia

This is a large family of climbers, but the easiest and quickest to grow is the *Bignonia rosa*, which grows a profusion of pale pink trumpet-shaped flowers through late summer into autumn. This climber is ideal for training over a car port or for somewhere that needs to be covered quickly. It is very strong and needs plenty of space to spread. The shoots must be tied to a support and secured as they grow. Prune back to old growth in November.

Another variety of bignonia is *Campsis radicans*, which has spectacular sprays of large orange-coloured trumpet-shaped flowers in summer. It is easy to grow and clings to walls by means of aerial roots.

Above *The rich orange-red flower of the bignonia campsis radicans in early summer.*
Right *The delicate pink trumpet-shaped flowers of the bignonia rosa. A vigorous climber, it will cover a wall or car port very quickly.*

Plumbago

This climber is very tolerant of heat and drought and can also be grown as a shrub or hedge, or allowed to cascade over terraces. It thrives in sun and semi-shade but is sensitive to frost. The most popular variety has clusters of powder blue flowers which bring a delightful coolness to the garden. The *Plumbago alba* has clusters of white flowers. A very effective way of covering a wall is to plant a blue plumbago next to a *Bignonia rosa*. Prune well after flowering.

Jasmine

Jasmines can be either shrubs or climbers, and the latter, if trained, can grow up to considerable heights. The common white jasmine has that wonderful heady scent which makes it perfect for planting around a door or patio, or where the smell can be most appreciated. It has small evergreen leaves and sprays of tiny, white, star-like flowers throughout summer and autumn, and often in spring. It is a rambling plant which needs support and will grow quite happily on a north wall. To keep a bushy

appearance, pinch out growing tips from time to time. It is resistant to drought and heat.

The yellow jasmine is a strong evergreen climber with no perfume. It can also be planted to grow over terraces, sending out strong shoots bearing single or double yellow flowers in late winter and early spring.

Below The most modest entrance can be transformed by exotic bougainvillea and sweet-scented jasmine.
Right *The bright orange-red, narrow tubular flowers of tecomaria capensis.*

Tecomaria capensis

This plant can be grown as a climber, hedge or shrub. It produces clusters of striking orange tubular flowers in summer through to autumn and has dark green glossy foliage. It likes full sun, standing up well to drought conditions. It dislikes frost and can be affected by cold winds when just about to flower. There is also a yellow variety.

Solanum

One of the best varieties in this family is *Solanum wendlandii*. This climber has a large leaf and beautiful clusters of powder blue flowers resembling those of the potato plant. It grows to a considerable height, its disadvantage being that it sheds its leaves at the end of the summer and is bare until the following spring. It is also well-liked by snails! These drawbacks apart, it will reward you with a beautiful show of flowers throughout the summer months. Partial sun and shade and a sheltered position suit the solanum.

Another species of solanum, which has small blue or white flowers with yellow centres, is *Solanum rantonnetii* – an excellent hardy climber that produces flowers from April through to November and is evergreen. It prefers a position of partial shade and grows rapidly.

Thunbergia *(Black-eyed Susan)*

There are many species of climbing or trailing plants in this group. They need very little attention and are often used for covering pergolas or car ports. *Thunbergia gibsonii* produces beautiful red-orange flowers in summer and autumn. *Thunbergia grandiflora* may be trained to climb up through trees and has blue flowers in clusters with yellow centres. They are vigorous growers and are ideal for areas that need quick cover.

Wisteria

The wisteria has been described as the queen of climbers, and with good reason. A well-established wisteria in full bloom in the spring, with its clusters of graceful pendulous flowers hanging beneath airy, delicate foliage, is a breathtaking sight.

Wisteria is in fact a fast-growing vine, and climbs by twisting around a support. It looks equally splendid trained over a pergola or archway, or climbing against a trellis or the wall of a house. The trunks and branches become gnarled and twisted as they age and add to the character of the plant. Growing a wisteria takes time and patience, but some things are worth waiting for.

This climber grows well in Spain as in many other countries. It thrives in a sheltered position in sun, but through experience I have found that exposure to full sun all day is just too much. Half sun and semi-shade often produce better results. When training leaders along a wall, try to keep them separated, otherwise they will twist around each other. Prune the vines in late summer when they are dormant, by shortening the previous year's growth by about one third. This will contain rampant growth and encourage good flowering shoots for the following year.

Pyracantha

This is a dark, evergreen climber which is covered in masses of tiny white flowers in spring and red or orange berries during autumn and winter. It is often slow to start but once established it grows rapidly, and is useful for covering an unsightly wall or corner. It is an extremely strong plant with stiff branches that bear sharp thorns, and withstands drought, hot winds, poor soil and hot sun. Pyracantha can be used for hedging, or as a climber or shrub and can be pruned to any shape. The best time for pruning is late autumn or early winter; shorten any long branches and cut out any dead wood.

Solandra

This is a delightful evergreen climber with large, glossy, mid-green leaves. On a south- or west-facing wall it can grow up to 5m (16ft) in any one year, and produces beautiful large golden-cup flowers with a scent reminiscent of ripe apricots from mid-January through to

Above *The exotic flower of the solandra, which has a scent reminiscent of ripe apricots.*
Left *A wisteria in full bloom always makes a spectacular sight with its trails of soft blue or white flowers.*
Far left *A cool, delicate colour scheme comprising the pale blue flowers of solanum wendlandii intertwined with white jasmine.*

Above *The deep blue flowers of ipomoea look most effective intertwined with those of bougainvillea, bignonia or honeysuckle.*

spring and intermittently throughout the year. It needs good support, but will survive strong sea breezes.

Lonicera *(Honysuckle)*

Honeysuckle grows well in Spain but in my experience prefers a shaded or a semi-shaded position. It is very useful for screening unsightly objects or areas, and it will also quite happily support itself on other plants. The small clusters of fine tubular flowers exude a wonderful perfume. It can grow rampant and is best cut back hard during the winter months to keep it in check.

Ipomoea *(Morning glory)*

Sow seeds of ipomoea in the spring near a wall or fence, or around the base of a bougainvillea so the plant will eventually intertwine with it. The seeds germinate very quickly and a strong-growing vine will shoot up to give a mass of brilliant sky-blue flowers throughout the summer. This is an annual climber and after the blooming season in autumn the plant will fade, but it is self-seeding and many new vines will appear the following season.

FLOWERING PLANTS

Perennial flowers are invaluable for the absentee gardener because, once planted, they require little attention (although they do need regular watering in dry spells) and will grow and spread each year. It is difficult to decide which is my favourite flower in Spain. In spring there are the beautiful freesias, anemones, irises, zantedeschias and amaryllis; from spring through to summer, the margaritas, cannas, roses, gazanias, and many many more. For the absentee gardener, I think my choice would have to be the geranium, which can be seen everywhere in Spain, tumbling over terraces, window boxes and pots in a bright profusion of pinks and reds. Geraniums grow all year round in Spain – I can recall being on a visit one February, when the geraniums were the best I had ever seen them.

Flowers grown in containers may be planted at any time of the year, except the hot summer months, and subject to weather and soil condi-

tions. Otherwise, the best times for planting are late autumn and early spring. Plant them in sunny, open areas where they will receive plenty of light.

Leave plenty of space between each plant to allow for growth and spreading, which are quite rapid in the Spanish climate. Dress with a balanced fertilizer in spring, and apply a mulch to conserve moisture in the soil. Dead-head regularly to encourage further blooms.

A selection of flowering plants is listed here in order of ease of cultivation.

Geranium
Geraniums can be planted almost anywhere, but they are at their best in a warm, sunny position. They flower profusely all year round

***Below** The bright flowers of geraniums always look at home in terracotta pots and will cheerfully put up with drought and poor soil.*

and are trouble-free – a definite boon for the absentee gardener.

Standard geraniums will often grow to a small bushy shrub, but take care not to let them become too straggly in appearance. The trailing varieties often have attractive variegated leaves, and will tumble over rocks, banks and walls, or climb up the trunks of trees and shrubs.

Geraniums are drought-resistant, but will respond well to weekly watering during the hottest months. Too much water, however, causes root rot. If the stems turn brown or black, remove the plant from the soil and take cuttings from young, green, healthy wood to make new plants.

Give a dressing of general fertilizer in the spring and spray with insecticide if greenfly are a problem. Dead-head regularly to stimulate new growth. For a particularly good show of flowers during the summer months, add a little liquid fertilizer once a month when watering.

Cacti and succulents

There are many species of cacti and succulents to choose from for your garden. All of them grow well in the hot climate of Spain with little, if any, attention. The flowers, though often short-lived, can be spectacular. These plants look striking when mixed together in groups with agaves and aloes. They make an eye-catching display grouped among old pots, gravel and coloured rocks as a corner feature in the garden or patio, or growing in pots on a paved area around your pool.

Dianthus

The dianthus family includes carnations, sweet williams and pinks. This is one of the easiest plants to grow in this region, thriving as it does

Below Cacti and succulents are fun, simple to grow, and will sometimes surprise you with an unexpected flower.

Above Chrysanthemum frutescens love the sun and flower for long spells during the summer months.

in the hot climate. Many of the dianthus family are fragrant, and make excellent border plants. The flowers range in colour from white to crimson, bright pink and yellow. They are an excellent choice for window boxes, and clumps of clove carnations planted in between geraniums give a magnificent show of colour throughout the summer months.

Chrysanthemum frutescens

There are many species in these families, all of which have a shrub-like nature that differs from that of the chrysanthemums sold as cut flowers by florists. Similar species are *dimorpothecas, anthemis* and *osteospermum*. They flower profusely in large clumps of small-to-medium sized, daisy-like flowers from spring through to late summer, provided they are dead-headed regularly. White is the predominant colour, but some species are yellow, pink, purple or red. The foliage can be bright green or grey-green and is often very fine.

Flowers in these groups will grow and multiply year after year. Propagate in the autumn by dividing the plant, making sure there is plenty of root attached for replanting.

Many Spanish garden centres group these daisy-like species together and call them 'margaritas'.

Canna

Cannas are bought as rhizomes and can be planted at any time from October to February. The very rich, tropical foliage grows to about 70cm (28in) high. The exotic flowers, resembling a cross between an orchid and a gladiolus, bloom throughout the summer months and

Right *Gazanias are excellent for planting in amongst rocks or on dry banks, where their bright yellow and orange flowers are shown to advantage throughout the summer months.*

Below *Cannas, with their handsome foliage and gaily coloured flowers, will grow equally well in a garden or in a container on a balcony or patio.*

occasionally right up to Christmas. The colours include red, yellow, pink and orange.

Cannas benefit from a good feed with manure or fertilizer in early spring, and need a certain amount of water during the summer months. The dead leaves and flowers should be trimmed throughout the season and cut down completely by the middle of February. They increase each year and can be split up and replanted in other areas of the garden.

Gazania *(Treasure flower)*
Gazanias grow to about 20cm (8in) high and thrive in full sun. The leaves are an attractive mid- or grey-green and the flowers are large and daisy-like, in colours ranging from yellow to orange, red and pink, as well as two-tone striped varieties. If you want a mass of sizzling colour in your garden in the summer months, group gazanias together with cannas.

Regular dead-heading keeps the flowers looking their best. Gazanias can be planted around the base of young trees, where they do well in dappled shade, or between young plants and shrubs that are slow to mature. There is also a trailing variety which is very useful as ground cover.

Agapanthus *(African lily)*

Agapanthus is a hardy perennial which grows prolifically in Australia, South Africa and South America, and also grows extremely well in Spain. The cool, pale blues, violet-blues and whites of the flowers offer a striking contrast to the bright oranges and reds of geraniums, cannas and other summer flowers.

Agapanthus have long, slender, fleshy leaves and large heads of tubular flowers borne at the ends of long stems in July and August. They will grow both in direct sunlight and in the more shady areas of your garden. They also thrive in outdoor containers in a sunny position.

Plant in mid spring, setting the rhizomes about 10cm (4in) below the surface. Do not disturb them after planting – they won't flower.

Below Agapanthus are exotic-looking flowers, yet they are easy to grow in sun or shade.

They respond well to regular watering, but will survive drought conditions. The seed pods which remain after flowering are excellent for dried flower arrangements.

Gerbera *(Transvaal daisy)*

Gerbera have large, daisy-like flowers in pale pinks, yellows and oranges, which are borne on 40cm (15in) long stems. They are excellent long-lasting flowers for cutting.

Plant in late autumn or early spring. Dig a hole big enough to allow the roots plenty of room to spread. Cover with a soil-and-compost mix. The crown of the plant should rest just above the soil surface. Make a ridge of soil around the plant to form a water-retaining basin. Water gently around the crown of the plant, trying not to wet the crown itself. Gerberas suffer from too much water. They thrive in a sunny, sheltered position, and need

Above *The white, waxen trumpets of the elegant arum lily, or Lily of the Nile.*

moderate watering. The long flower stems may need some support against strong winds.

Zantedeschia *(Arum lily)*

These perennial plants grow well in full sun or partial shade and need water during dry spells. They have exotic mid-green leaves and beautiful, white, trumpet-shaped flowers. If you leave the rhizomes in the soil after the flowers fade, the leaves will turn yellow and they will multiply and flower again next season. After flowering leave to dry out during the summer months. Resume watering during September or October, when the new shoots will start to grow for the following spring flowering.

Aeonium

Aeonium are striking plants producing large, thick yellow flower heads during early spring. They have thick, blue-grey succulent rosette-shaped leaves. Like cacti they mix well with aloes and agaves, and are best planted in cracks in walls or among rocks. They love the

sun and need very little attention apart from dead-heading through the year.

Rose

Roses grow beautifully in Spain but they do need a certain amount of attention and if you do not spend much time in your holiday home during the year it is probably wiser to plant other, more hardy plants. However, if you do decide to plant roses in your garden there are many different kinds to choose from. The most useful are the large-flowered hybrid teas and the cluster-flowered floribundas, which bloom from late spring and throughout the summer months. Most of these are fragrant. Some are more disease-resistant than others – your garden centre will be able to advise. They need well-drained, fertile soil, plenty of water, particularly in the summer months, regular feeding and plenty of light. Roses also need to be protected from strong winds; they do best in a sheltered, undisturbed atmosphere.

For the absentee gardener it is advisable to buy container-grown roses, which can be planted in spring and autumn, provided they can be kept well watered until established. Dig the hole for the container and mix in some potting compost and manure, taking care that the manure does not come into contact with the roots. Firm the soil around the bush to prevent the rose from being 'rocked' by the wind. Water generously, repeating a few days later. (See pages 24–25 for more detailed instructions on planting.)

January is the best time to prune roses in Spain. Cut out all old, weak, diseased or damaged stems. Then shorten strong remaining shoots to an outward facing bud; the weaker the stems the harder you should prune. Give a good dressing of manure after pruning. Spring is also the time to spray with a fungicide and insecticide, if necessary. For beautiful, healthy plants, it is worth spraying at six-weekly intervals throughout the growing season. When watering, an addition of liquid fertilizer from time to time will help to produce better blooms.

GROUND COVER PLANTS

Low-growing, spreading, ground cover plants are not only decorative in their own right; they also fulfil a number of useful functions around the garden. Once planted, they establish a dense, weed-smothering carpet within a season or two, thus helping to keep weeding chores to a minimum. They are also invaluable for covering up areas of bare soil in patches of shade or between newly-planted shrubs and trees. They are excellent for retaining soil on sloping banks and terraces, for softening the straight edges of paths and driveways, and for trailing over walls, pots and window boxes.

Ground cover plants require little or no maintenance beyond occasional dead-heading and cutting back.

Lantana

There are several varieties of lantana which are excellent for ground cover and will provide good displays of colour (red, yellow and purple) throughout the summer. Dead-head the flowers regularly to stimulate new growth.

Lantana thrives in hot, sunny conditions and looks delightful tumbling over a wall.

Mesembryanthemum *(Ice plants)*

There are well over a thousand species in this group, including Doreanthus (Livingstone daisy), Lampranthus, Carpobrutus and Ruschia. These plants are all extremely useful for the absentee gardener as they thrive in hot, dry, sunny conditions. They are characterized by their fleshy, succulent-type leaves and brilliantly coloured daisy-like flowers.

Carpobrutus has bright pink or yellow flowers and long, pointed, grey-green fleshy leaves. It grows profusely anywhere and is suitable for trailing over terraces or on steep banks, ensuring that soil is not washed away by heavy rain. It is known locally in Spain as 'Una de Leon'.

Below *Ruschia is a useful, very fast-growing ground cover plant with bright green fleshy leaves and tiny pink flowers.*

Ruschia has tiny pink or yellow flowers and bright green, flat, fleshy leaves. It is excellent for quick ground cover and survives well with little attention. Occasionally in particularly dry conditions the leaves may begin to turn yellow. If this does occur, thin out the plants and remove discoloured stems and leaves. Water well; they will soon recover.

In some garden centres in Spain there may be confusion about the names of the various ground cover plants in this group. If you ask for Mesembryanthemums ('Mesems') or ice plants ('Flor de Cucaillo') which are general terms for low-growing, succulent-type plants producing brilliantly coloured daisy-shaped flowers, you should be able to find the plants described and illustrated.

Portulaca

Portulaca is a summer annual with small narrow fleshy leaves which suits a position in full sun. The brilliant flowers (red, pink, orange, yellow and white) open when the sun shines and close when it moves away and the flowers are left in the shade. Sow seeds where you wish them to grow. They tolerate drought and will self-seed year after year.

Verbena

This is a very useful and attractive plant for ground cover. The flowers appear at the tips of the stems in small, flat clusters of red, pink, salmon, purple and white, and the feathery leaves are medium-to-dark green. They spread quickly and groups of three or more plants will carpet a large area. The best show of flowers is in the spring, but if the plant is watered and trimmed from time to time they will last right through to the autumn. When the weather becomes too cold or too hot the plants can turn brown, but quickly recover after a short spell of watering. They are ideal for edging, for container growing, and for trailing over rocks or terraces.

SPRING-FLOWERING BULBS

Spring-flowering bulbs, corms and tubers give maximum reward for minimum effort, making them a must for the absentee gardener. They can be planted in October or November (even as early as the last week of September) when many visitors to Spain are closing their summer homes for the winter months, and give a spectacular show of colour from the end of January through to early May. Most of them can remain in the ground after flowering and will go on producing lovely flowers, year after year.

Bulbs are also very versatile. They will grow in either sun or light shade and are not fussy about soil. Grow them in clumps to edge your pool, in groups amongst rocks or on terraces, or around the base of trees and shrubs. They are also excellent flowers for the balcony or patio.

Amaryllis

The amaryllis is a beautiful and unusual plant, with large, trumpet-shaped flowers in brilliant red, yellow or pinky-white. The bulbs are rather expensive to buy, but a group of two or three planted together among low-growing shrubs looks most impressive.

Plant the bulbs in a warm, sheltered place. Line the planting hole with a little compost and cover the bulb up to its neck in soil. After flowering allow the foliage to die right down and trim off when quite dry.

Anemone

This is another valuable spring flower that looks most attractive planted in groups or at the base of trees and shrubs. The plants produce single or double flowers in brilliant, jewel-like colours – white, red, pink, blue and purple – with large black centres. The bright green, feathery foliage is also attractive.

It is advisable to soak the corms overnight in warm water to get them started into growth. Plant 2·5cm (1in) deep in a compost and soil mix and water generously.

Clivia

Clivias are beautiful plants for shady areas of the garden and are particularly suitable for

Left The magnificent, lily-like flower of amaryllis can also be found in dark red, orange, apple-blossom pink and white.
Far left Verbena is a dainty, attractive ground cover and trailing plant that will clothe a wall or a bare area of the garden very quickly.

growing in containers on balconies or patios. They have thick, tuberous roots which produce glossy, dark green leaves. Clusters of exotic orange flowers are produced on short, thick stems in late winter and early spring. The cut flowers are long lasting. Add a good dressing of manure in the autumn to ensure good growth and flower production in the following spring. Water from time to time during the hot summer months. The tubers will multiply each year and can be lifted and divided after flowering. Plant 35–40cm (12–16in) apart, with the crowns well above soil level.

Cyclamen

Cyclamen planted in groups under a deciduous tree in semi-shade make a spectacular sight in late winter and early spring. They are tuberous-rooted plants and can be left in the ground for many seasons to multiply and produce a regular show of flowers each year. The heart-shaped foliage is also most decorative. Dress the soil around the plants with compost when flowering is over, to help protect the plants from drying out in the hot summer months.

Freesia

Freesias are wonderfully fragrant flowers, which makes them excellent as cut flowers for indoors. The colourful blooms (white, pink, yellow, orange, red and mauve) come in single or double form and are borne on 20–45cm (8–18in) high delicate stems.

Plant freesias in groups so that the tops of the bulbs are just below the surface. They thrive in sun or half-shade, and their fragrant flowers provide a carpet of colour each March. They may need to be lightly staked when they reach full height. The bulbs can be left in the ground to multiply, and produce many bulblets, which flower after two or three years. Alternatively they can be lifted, dried and stored for planting the following year.

Right An enclosed patio with pots of clivia massed in the foreground. Their showy heads of orange and yellow make a welcome sight in spring.

Iris

Iris grow well and flower profusely during the spring. They are best planted in groups, and the purple, white, blue or bi-coloured, flag-shaped flowers make a particularly attractive backdrop for geraniums or zantedeschias.

Arrange the rhizomes so they all face the same way – leaf-shoot end away from the sun. Plant so that the top of the rhizome is just visible above the soil. Dead-head during the flowering season and tidy the leaves and stalks after flowering. Do not over-water.

Below *The pale lilac flags of the iris give a beautiful display in early spring.*

Ranunculus

These hardy, tuberous-rooted perennials have double or semi-double flowers in a wide range of bright colours and are excellent for cutting. They combine particularly well with anemones.

Plant the claw-shaped tubers with their points down 2·5cm (1in) deep and 10cm (4in) apart in a sunny position sheltered from the wind. Add potting compost to the planting mixture and water well. Ranunculus need regular watering and feeding before the buds open. When the plants have died down, lift and store dried corms in sand or sawdust ready for planting the following year.

PLANTS FOR THE
LONG-TERM VISITOR

All of the plants I've described so far in this chapter have been chosen for their ability to grow successfully in the hot, dry climate of Spain with a minimum of maintenance and watering. However, if you are a permanent resident in Spain, or are planning to be in the country for extended periods, there is no reason at all why you should not grow an even wider range of flowers and plants. Hardy and half-hardy annuals; bulbs; flowers for cutting and for drying; container plants – all of these will grow well in Spain provided you are able to give them the regular attention they need, such as staking, trimming, cutting, watering and feeding.

What to plant in the winter

If you intend to spend the winter months in Spain, say between October and March, you can plant bulbs in containers or in the garden at the beginning of October. Dress them with a little fertilizer and they can then be left alone to produce a beautiful show of flowers in the following spring.

Shrubs and roses can also be planted in October: this will give them a chance to get well established before their first growing season. Be sure to incorporate plenty of organic matter into the soil when planting, as this will act as a sponge and help to retain water during the dry months. Sweet peas can be planted between October and January and will often self-seed and appear the following year.

February is the time to plant gladioli, dahlias and begonias – though do so only if they are going to be adequately watered in summer.

Pruning of established shrubs and roses can be done at any time between October and the end of January, and if you are planning to lay a new lawn, now is the best time. If you would like to try your hand at growing a few vegetables, broad beans and peas planted in October will be ready to eat at Easter.

The winter winds in the coastal regions of southern Spain can be very strong and often cold, and can damage vulnerable trees and climbers; an afternoon in the autumn devoted to examining supports and ties, and renewing them if necessary, will be time well spent. Finally, a good dressing of manure or compost around the base of plants, trees and shrubs will enrich the soil and encourage strong, healthy growth in the spring.

What to plant in the summer

If you are staying at your villa or apartment from March to September, you can sow any number of summer hardy annuals. These are easy to grow, asking only a place in the sun and water in dry weather, and will set your garden ablaze with colour from early summer until autumn.

Seeds germinate very quickly in the warm Spanish spring. They can be sown directly in the ground where they are to flower, or you can start them off early in pots or boxes. Protect the emerging seedlings against the cold mornings and evenings of early spring by covering the boxes with a sheet of polythene.

You can also grow your own vegetables from seed if you fancy. Although tomatoes, broad beans, peas and artichokes are cheap and plentiful in Spanish shops and markets, there is nothing to beat the pleasure of growing your own. Besides, the bright fruits and lush green foliage will add colour to a garden or, if grown in pots, a sunny balcony.

Everyone has their own favourite annuals, such as godetia, salvia, antirrhinums, stocks and marigolds. The list is too numerous to mention in the scope of this book, but on the following pages I have suggested a few that are

colourful, easy to grow, and, in many cases, that will provide cut flowers for indoors.

Begonia

The tuberous begonia has showy blooms in a wide range of yellows, oranges, pinks and reds, often combined with attractive foliage. It is ideal for adding summer colour to pots, window boxes and borders, and the pendulous variety is a stunning sight when cascading from a hanging basket.

Plant the tuber in early spring, hollow side facing up. Alternatively, buy established plants from a garden centre or market and plant in early summer. Arrange in groups, setting each plant 20cm (8in) apart.

Begonias are happy in light shade or sun. Water regularly in summer, but take care not to soak the crown of the plant.

Dahlia

These are tuberous-rooted tender perennials, flowering from early summer through to late autumn. The flowers come in numerous forms, and the extensive colour range includes red, pink, purple, yellow, orange, white and cream. They average 1–2m (3–6ft) in height, though there is also a dwarf bedding variety. Dahlias make excellent cut flowers for the home.

Plant tubers 40–60cm (16–24in) apart in February or March, mixing a little compost with the soil. Dahlias grow best in a moist, well-drained, fertile soil. They love the sun, but must be generously watered during the summer. They also appreciate an application of liquid feed once a week during the flowering season.

Dwarf varieties need no support, but standard dahlias must be staked to protect them from strong winds. They are susceptible to attack by aphids, so spray with insecticide when the new shoots appear and at regular intervals afterwards. When the plant has three

Left and above *The single dahlia and the double pompon variety. Both have a long flowering period but need regular watering.*

or four leaves, pinch out the top leaves to encourage a stronger plant. When buds appear at the top of a branch, pinch off the side buds: this encourages a strong bud to grow and produces a larger flower.

When the plant has died down in the autumn and the leaves have turned yellow and black, cut the main stem to within 15cm (6in) of the tuber. Lift the tuber, wipe it completely free of soil, and leave it upside down in a dry place for a few days. Then dust with sulphur and store in an aerated box in a cool, dry, frost-free cupboard or shed.

Fuchsia

There are many species of fuchsia, some hardy, some half-hardy and some very tender. Some hardy species can be trained as a bush or standard. There are many beautiful colour combinations, in a range of pinks, whites and reds. They flower at different times all year round, and it is possible to have fuchsias in full flower in your garden in January. They are also excel-

Above Fuchsias are ideal for growing in pots, window boxes and hanging baskets if you are visiting your holiday home for a long spell.

lent for container growing.

Fuchsias look particularly attractive planted slightly above eye level, so that the undersides of the pendulous flowers can be appreciated. They need a well-drained, sheltered position in semi-shade. Take care not to plant in full sun.

Plant in early autumn or mid-spring, about 60cm (24in) apart. Add a good potting compost to the soil and water well. During the growing season add a dressing of compost or manure and feed regularly for best results. Throughout the growing season fuchsias need regular dead-heading. Pinch out the growing tips from time to time to encourage new growth. The flowers are produced on young wood.

Impatiens *(Busy Lizzie)*

Impatiens, better known as Busy Lizzie, is a superb half-hardy annual, excellent for summer bedding and borders. The double flowers, in shades of red, white and pink, bloom from early summer through to autumn. It is best planted in light shade or in a position that receives the early morning sun.

Sow seeds in spring in a sunny situation and thin out when the seedlings reach 6cm (2in)

high. Water freely and apply liquid feed during the flowering season. They may successfully be grown from stem cuttings at any time.

Gladiolus *(Sword lily)*

Gladioli have sword-shaped leaves and long spikes of trumpet-shaped flowers. These ele-

Right Gladioli in full bloom. The tapering spikes of flowers are excellent for cutting and come in a bewildering range of colours and forms.
Below An impressive massed display of impatiens.

gant, showy flowerheads make gladioli popular as a garden plant and for cutting. They come in a wide range of flower shapes and colours.

Gladioli grow best in fertile, well-drained soil in a sunny position. They can be planted in October and November for spring flowering, or in February and March for summer flowering. Plant the corms 8–10cm (3–4in) deep on a bed of sand-and-compost mix. Cover and water well. Set the corms in clumps 10–15cm (4–6in) apart, or in rows 30–38 (12–15in) apart.

Water well during flowering and give liquid feeds regularly. Tall varieties may need staking. Groups of gladioli can look most attractive if planted in a circle and tied to three or four canes positioned in the centre for support.

Lift the corms in the autumn. Cut off the main stem 1cm (½in) above the corm, then leave to dry for a week or so. Store in shallow boxes in a cool, dry, frost-proof place. Remove the old corms from the base of the new ones.

Gloxinia

These are tender tuberous-rooted plants with dark green, velvety leaves and trumpet-shaped, brilliantly coloured flowers which appear in late summer in red, purple, blue, pink, white and mixed colours.

Plant the tuber in a hole not more than 5cm (2in) deep, lined with a mixture of potting compost and soil. Cover gently and water lightly until the first leaves appear. Gloxinias need plenty of water and shade from hot sun, but when watering, take care not to wet the leaves. After flowering the tubers should be lifted, dried off and stored for the winter in a cool place.

Helianthus *(Sunflower)*

This is a popular and hardy plant, usually grown as an annual, although some are perennial. Sunflowers bloom from June through to August, producing huge, plate-shaped yellow flowers with black seed rings in the centre. They grow very quickly, some reaching up to 2m (6ft) high, and the flowers can be anything from 7–30cm (3–12in) across. There are also dwarf varieties, which, if dead-headed regularly, will continue flowering all through the summer. The flowers turn to follow the sun's progress through the sky each day.

These are excellent plants, whether used as bedding display or as a splash of background colour. They thrive in full sun, provided they receive some water during the hottest summer months. If you are growing a newly planted hedge such as cupressus or myporem, you can plant sunflower seeds in between the hedging plants. These will help to fill in the gaps until the hedge becomes more established.

Sunflowers are easy and fun to grow. Soak the seeds in warm water overnight and then sow them in holes 3–4cm (1–2in) deep and 50cm (20in) apart, three to four seeds to a hole, in a sunny position in late spring where the plants are to flower. Water well and cover with a soil-and-compost mix. As the seedlings develop, thin them out, saving only the strongest plants. As they grow they will need to be

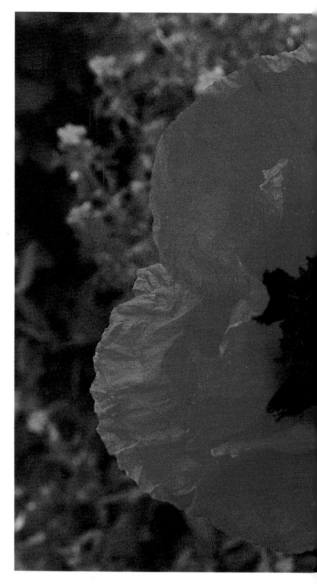

staked or tied to a fence to prevent them falling over, either because of the wind or the weight of the flower head.

If you want to collect the edible seeds, cover them with a piece of gauze tied to the stem as soon as they start to ripen, to protect the seeds from the birds.

Petunia

These colourful annuals are excellent for planting in groups to 'fill in' areas of your

garden, and can also be grown in tubs and window boxes. They are most effective planted around the base of trees and shrubs. Their trumpet-shaped flowers can be single, double or frilled, and come in a wide range of colours.

Sow seeds indoors in early spring and plant outdoors 25cm (9in) apart in early summer. Alternatively, buy young bedding plants from a market or garden centre. Petunias like a rich, sandy loam and a sunny situation, and require regular watering in summer.

Above *The huge, bowl-shaped blooms of oriental poppies give a dazzling display in summer.*

Poppy

Poppies are always a popular choice for the garden, their brightly coloured flowers borne on tall stems blooming throughout the summer. Iceland poppies supply superb cut flowers as well as a lasting garden display.

Sow seeds 1–2mm (1/16in) deep in March or April. Water regularly during dry spells.

Sweet pea

The sweet pea is a hardy annual, fragrant and beautifully coloured in a range of delicate pastel shades. They are mostly climbing plants, but there are also dwarf varieties for massing and bedding, and for window boxes. Sweet peas will bloom throughout the summer in a sunny, sheltered spot.

Sweet pea seeds must be soaked overnight in warm water before planting, to encourage germination. Sow them in October and November, or February and March, 5cm (2in) deep and 8cm (3in) apart, in deeply-dug, rich soil. Protect the emerging shoots on cold nights by lightly covering with pine needles or dry leaves. Pinch out the growing tips when the second set of leaves has formed, to encourage side shoots.

Sweet peas must be watered regularly, especially in hot, dry periods. Grow them in rows or clumps and supply wire netting, canes or a trellis on walls and fences for support. If the flowers are picked each day, blooming will be more prolific.

Zinnia

Zinnias flower best in full sun, and their gaily coloured blooms last for many weeks. They grow up to 40–50cm (16–20in) tall and make

Above and below Sweet peas (above) and zinnias (below) love the sun, are long-lasting, come in a wide range of colours – and are easy to grow.

excellent cut flowers. Miniature zinnias can be grown in tubs and window boxes, planted among geraniums and dianthus.

Sow seed in February and March. Thin out to 5cm (2in) apart and water well. Transplant in early summer, spacing the plants 20–30cm (8–12in) apart. It is best to transplant young seedlings in late afternoon, when they can be well watered without fear of being scorched by the hot sun. They need regular watering during summer.

FLOWERS FOR
DRIED ARRANGEMENTS

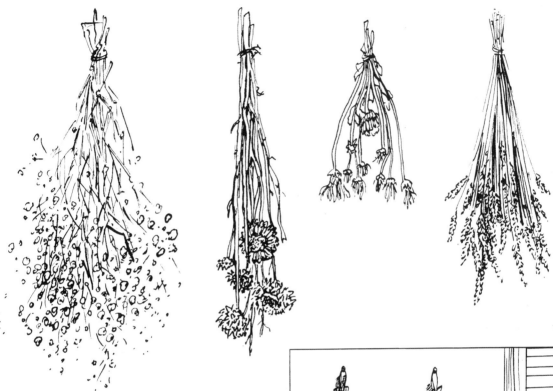

The climate in Spain is ideal for drying flowers, and they are very easy to grow. Sow the seeds in March or April in a seed bed, either in drills or in small circles or rectangles. Water well until they germinate. When large enough to handle, transfer the seedlings to a separate flower bed or plant around shrubs and trees, about 5–10cm (2–4in) apart.

Cut the flowers when still fresh, remove most of the foliage, and group them into bunches of not more than four to six stems, so that air can circulate freely between them. Tie the bunches fairly tightly with string or raffia and suspend them, heads downwards, in a dry, well-ventilated room, away from direct light, until dry and ready to use.

Use a ventilated paper bag to catch seeds.

Achillea filipendulina *(Yarrow)*

This is a very attractive plant for flower decoration. It is a perennial and has fine, fern-like, greyish leaves and a yellow, circular flower head. Achillea is a strong grower and tolerates intense heat and frost, full sun and poor soil. Pick only the best flowers, strip off the leaves and hang to dry.

Helichrysum

This is the most commonly used flower in dried arrangements. The blooms are small, straw-like daisies and their vibrant colours – crimson, pink, orange, scarlet and white – stay bright and never fade.

Always harvest the flowers before they have fully opened, and hang them upside down in a cool, dry place. If the stems stiffen and dry out completely, attach some thin green florists' wire to the back of the head of the flower, bending the wire to make an artificial stem.

Lavender

This lovely, traditional herb needs no introduction. Lavender spikes should be cut when about half of the flowers are open. Pick the flowers when fresh in bloom; do not wait for them to fade before you dry them.

Lunaria *(Honesty)*

Lunaria has light and dark purple flowers which are not particularly attractive; however the circular, silvery, parchment-like seed pods produced after flowering are a must for indoor decoration, either mixed with other dried

flowers or grouped en masse in a brightly coloured Spanish vase. Lunaria grows very easily – so easily, in fact, that it will spread to other parts of your garden if you do not keep it in check.

Nigella damascena

Nigella, better known as 'love-in-a-mist', has feathery green foliage and flowers similar in appearance to cornflowers, in blue, white purple or pink. They begin to bloom in June and last all summer. By September the flower heads have become circular seed pods covered in tiny spikes. Both the flowers and the seed pods are most effective when dried. Be sure to shake the seed pods to release the seeds, which you can save for planting the following year.

Statice sinuata

Statice sinuata likes a sunny position and can be grown around the base of trees and shrubs. It grows to a height of 30–40cm (12–16in) and produces long-lasting sprays of blue, yellow, pink, lavender or white flowers, which are a favourite with flower arrangers. Seeds sown in the open germinate in 10–15 days.

Far left Achillea are popular summer border plants, and some are also suitable for rock gardens or dry walls. All will thrive in sunny, open areas.
Left The showy flower heads of helichrysum are extremely popular for dried arrangements.

CULINARY HERBS

During recent years there has been a dramatic revival of interest in herbs, due partly to the growth in popularity of Mediterranean cuisine and partly as a reaction against the bland, synthetic, over-processed foods that make up so much of the Western diet today.

Herbs have always featured strongly in Mediterranean cooking, and are appreciated for their nutritional and healing properties as well as for their flavour. So, when in Spain,

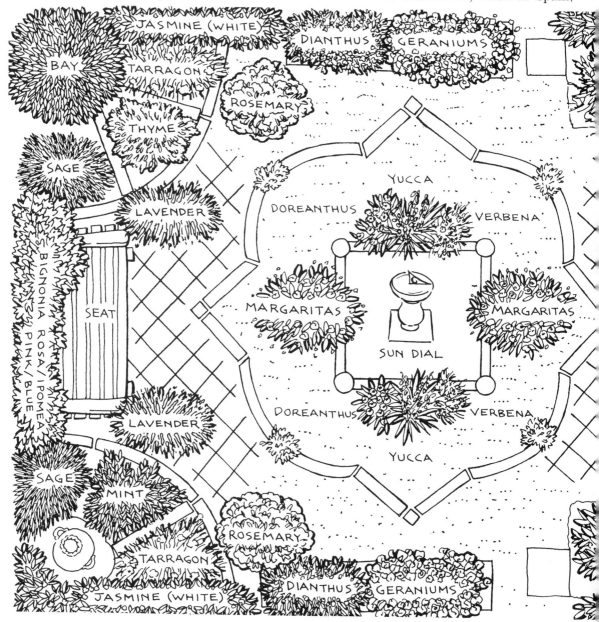

why not do as the Spanish do? Growing your own herbs is easy and fun, and will add a whole new dimension to your cooking. An excellent way of barbecue cooking, for example, is to add branches of thyme or rosemary to the coals; the flavour permeates the meat during cooking, and the smell that wafts across the garden is enough to send the taste buds into overdrive!

You don't need 'green fingers', or lots of space or time, to grow herbs. Many herbs have Mediterranean origins, so they thrive in strong sunshine and poor soil, and require little or no attention. Grow them in a corner of the garden near your kitchen or barbecue area, or along with other shrubs and plants in a sunny position. If space is short, you can grow them in pots on a balcony or terrace: even if you have room to grow only parsley, thyme and bay, you have the three herbs which are used in a *bouquet garni,* the traditional 'herb posy' which adds such rich flavouring to stews and sauces.

Herb gardens

If you're an enthusiastic cook, or simply a herb-lover, you may want to create a little herb garden close to the house. This could be a fancy affair along the lines of a formal English herb garden, with narrow tiled paths running through it for easy access. Or it could be as simple as an old ladder or cartwheel laid on the ground, with different herbs planted between the spokes. One simple but effective design is a chequerboard of large terracotta tiles with herbs planted in every other square. At the centre of your herb garden you could position an arbour, an antique pot, a sundial or a seat, from which to appreciate the smells of the herbs.

Rosemary, thyme, sage, tarragon, marjoram, parsley, mint, garlic and bay are the most useful and resilient herbs for the absentee gardener to grow.

All these herbs, apart from garlic, are best bought as plants in containers and planted 30–45cm (12–16in) apart in the early spring.

To encourage compact, bushy plants, tip-prune by pinching out the small growing tip or bud. If plants become leggy, prune back well in the autumn.

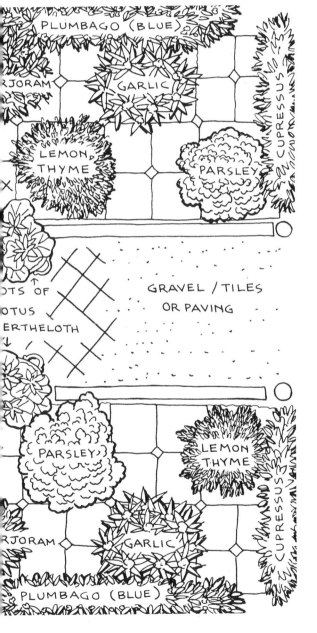

Left *Suggested plan for a large herb garden, sections could be adapted to make smaller schemes.*

Bay

This is a perennial evergreen shrub, the leaves of which are widely used in cooking. Bay leaves are shiny, smooth and dark, with a strong aromatic scent, and can be picked throughout the year.

Bay trees can be clipped and pruned to make ornamental shapes and are ideal for container growing. They will grow more successfully in areas of light shade; too much hot Spanish sun can scorch the leaves.

Bay is one of the three herbs used in the *bouquet garni*, used to flavour Mediterranean dishes. It will add a spicy flavour to marinades, and to tomato dishes and casseroles. Remove the leaves before serving.

Marjoram

Marjoram is simple to grow and will thrive in a sunny position provided it is watered from time to time during the hot summer months. It grows about 30–60cm (12–24in) high and is strongly aromatic. Add to tomato dishes, stews, pasta dishes and soups.

Garlic

Garlic is a perennial herb of the onion family. For best results, plant in rich, moist soil in an open, sunny position. Plant individual cloves of garlic in December or January, set 15cm (6in) apart, with the tips just level with the soil surface. Water well in dry spells. When the leaves begin to turn yellow, lift the garlic and leave it to dry in the sun. Tie in bunches and hang in a cool, dry place.

Used sparingly, garlic improves the flavour of just about any meat or vegetable dish. Try rubbing a cut clove around the bowl used for a green salad.

Mint

This herb is best grown in the shade and needs watering from time to time in dry spells. It spreads rapidly by means of underground runners: plant it in a sunken, bottomless container if you want to prevent it from taking over the entire garden.

Use mint to make a sauce to accompany roast lamb, or to flavour peas and new potatoes. Chopped and added to yoghurt, it goes well with spicy foods. Make a cooling mint water ice or add to fruit juices. It also makes a delicious tea which is surprisingly refreshing in a hot climate.

Parsley

No herb garden is complete without parsley, as it is the most widely used of all herbs. The flat-leaved Spanish or Italian parsley grows thick and fast, and is best thinned by pulling it out by the root. Some people prefer the curly variety, which does not spread so quickly. If your parsley goes to seed in your absence, cut it down to about 5cm (2in) from the ground and it will soon grow new shoots.

The flat-leaved parsley has a pleasant, nutty flavour and is excellent in green salads. Both types of parsley can be added to soups, sauces and fish dishes, and curly parsley makes an attractive garnish. Parsley also softens the flavour of dishes that contain garlic.

Rosemary

Rosemary has always grown wild around the Mediterranean coasts, where it thrives on the harsh limestone soils. It can grow up to 1m (3ft) high, but is very slow-growing. A dwarf variety, 45cm (18in) high, is suitable where space is limited, or for container growing. The leaves are short, narrow and tough, and small grey-blue flowers are borne in summer. The whole plant has a strong aromatic smell.

Rosemary with lamb is an old favourite, but it also goes well with chicken or fish dishes.

Sage

This herb thrives well in shade or semi-shade, growing into a small evergreen bush 60–120cm (2–4ft) high. If it becomes untidy, cut the woody branches hard back from time to time. The leaves are a pale grey-green, with a rough texture. The flowers are a soft purple.

Sage is an aid to digestion, and has traditionally been used in stuffings for pork, duck, goose and turkey. Chopped sage also goes well with liver and cheese dishes.

Tarragon

Tarragon thrives in a sunny, sheltered position, but for the absentee gardener, a position in semi-shade will probably produce the best results. It grows between 60–100cm (24–40in) in height and bears tiny, greenish-white flowers and shiny, narrow leaves.

Make tarragon vinegar by steeping sprigs of the fresh herb in white wine vinegar. Tarragon can be added in small quantities to poultry dishes, fish and salads.

Thyme

Thyme is a low-growing, spreading, evergreen shrub bearing tiny mauve flowers in early summer. It will grow in any sunny position and is equally suitable for container growing.

Shoots of thyme required for seasoning should be gathered as soon as the flowers appear. Use them fresh, or tie them in small bundles and hang them head downwards in a cool, airy place.

Thyme has a fairly strong flavour and can be added to stuffings for veal and poultry.

LAWNS

You are probably familiar with two ways of making a lawn – laying turf or sowing seed. In Spain, however, grass is most often bought in the form of little clumps of root, known as stolons. In a hot climate, grass will grow much more successfully if planted by root than by seed. There are two main types of lawn grass to choose from. For a hardwearing lawn that needs the minimum of attention, *Grama* grass is perhaps the best type to buy. It is tough and resilient, and quickly spreads across the surface of the soil. An alternative type of grass, which gives a much smoother lawn and is used on most golf courses, is a variety of *Agrostis*. If you are undecided about which type to buy, consult your local garden centre for advice.

For best results, plant your lawn in spring or early autumn. Mark out the area and dig over the ground, removing stones, rocks and debris. Work in some good quality topsoil; this should be 10–15cm (4–6in) deep for a good lawn. Rake over, then apply a dressing of super phosphate and general fertilizer. Roll the soil well, until you are satisfied that you have a level surface. Water late in the day to settle and moisten the soil ready for planting the following morning.

Mark out a number of furrows across the whole of the lawn area, 7cm (3in) deep and 10cm (4in) apart. Plant the stolons in the furrows, 10cm (4in) apart, and cover the roots with soil as you go. Finish by rolling first in one direction and then in the opposite direction. Give the soil a thorough soaking, and again during the evening. Keep the area thoroughly watered until the grass is established, and continue to do so throughout the first season.

As the grass begins to grow, trim it gently with shears. Leave the clippings on the soil – they often contain seed and this will help to produce a thicker lawn in a shorter space of time.

For the first mowing, set the blades of your mower in the highest position possible, then adjust as the lawn becomes established.

During the summer months a good soaking twice a week will be more beneficial than a spray once a day. Water in the early morning or late evening. A lawn needs to be top-dressed and fertilized periodically throughout the year. If you have a weed problem, apply a lawn weedkiller in early spring or autumn – never in the hot summer months, as the grass is likely to turn brown.

Left A lawn planted up to the edge of a swimming pool. As the photograph illustrates, it is difficult to maintain a lush green sward in such a hot climate!

COLOUR AND SCENT
IN YOUR GARDEN

Planning the colours of your plants to complement each other, or to create contrast, is perhaps the most difficult part of creating a garden, particularly as different flowers bloom at different times of the year.

Start by planning your colours in seasons and work from there. For example, you can be sure your mimosa tree will bloom profusely each February to March with a splash of yellow. Groups of spring flowers such as freesias, amaryllis, anemones, daffodils, hyacinths, and, later, tulips will add bright reds, yellows, blues and pinks. White margaritas and the ever-present pink and red geraniums will also be in flower. Oranges and lemons will be on your trees. To complement and offset these bright colours you could plant grey-green or variegated agaves, a pine or a carob, and the different greens of shrubs can also be positioned to break up the splashes of bright colour.

From April the lavender blue wisteria is in bloom, and in the month of May many of the other climbers are at their best: think of the brilliant pinks and purples of bougainvilleas, the soft powder blue of the *Solanum wendlandii*, the plumbago, as well as the lavender-blue jacaranda. This profusion of colour will last right through to the end of June or early July, which is the best time of the year for oleanders, hibiscus and many of the flowering shrubs.

From June and throughout the summer months, the brilliant oranges, reds and yellows of cannas and gazanias appear, making a striking contrast with the blues and whites of agapanthus.

During the hot months you can perhaps plan a cool, shady corner, planting a datura, two or three lavender bushes and, in the background, a clump of bright green bamboo, a dark-leaved bay tree or a white climber such as jasmine or *Solanum rantonnetii*.

In early September most of the summer flowers have passed their peak, but the white plumes of pampas grass will be a feature and the bougainvilleas will still be brilliant. The pale pink of *Bignonia rosa* will complement the soft September evenings.

Throughout the year, Canary palms, agaves and yuccas will provide lush greens to contrast with and complement the bright colours of flowers. The wispy green leaves of schinus or bamboo will move gently in the breeze, creating a cooling effect.

From mid-October the bright orange flowers of the aloe, perhaps planted in a dry, dull corner, will come into bloom and in December the bright red flowers (or bracts to be more specific) of the poinsettia will remind you of Christmas back home!

Colour combinations in your garden

It is important to think of the various colour combinations of your plants, and well thought out colour groupings can be used to great effect. Creams, pale yellows and blues will create a look of space and make your garden, or an area of your garden, look larger. The same effect can be created with pale pinks combined with grey-green foliage. Purples, lilacs, pale blues and pinks can also give a soft, restful effect. Add a touch of sharpness by including the acid green of wisteria leaves or the bright green leaves of bamboo.

Whites, creams and grey-green foliage grouped around a shady paved area of the garden can create a cool, restful corner away from the unrelenting heat of the summer sun.

Bright reds, oranges and yellows are best kept towards the front of a group of plants, as they stand out in any garden design. A group of brilliant red and orange flowers will be given more depth if planted together with whites, paler creams and yellows.

Massing colours in groups is much more effective than planting single specimens dotted in between others all over the garden, although this is easier to do in a large garden than in a small one. Plant shrubs in clumps of three or more to fill out large spaces or to attract the eye in the centre of a lawn; oleanders and hibiscus are particularly effective planted in this way, as are hybrid tea roses. If you want a splash of bright colour, try planting red cannas in front of datura in full bloom. For a shady corner, clumps of blue agapanthus close to a group of white geraniums create a restrained and elegant effect.

For a small garden, it is often wise to limit your colours to a few restful, pale pinks, whites or blues, mixed with grey or dark green foliage. Try a combination of *Bignonia rosa,* pale pink geraniums, white jasmine and pink oleander, offset by a pale blue plumbago and two or three cupressus in different shades of green.

These examples are, of course, simplified, and colour is very much a matter of personal taste, but they will give you some ideas to start off with.

The scented garden

To have a garden filled with colourful blooms is indeed a pleasure, but if you neglect to consider fragrance, too, you are missing out on one of the joys of gardening. In Spain you will find an excellent choice of scented flowers, herbs and shrubs that fill the air with a heady perfume or exude a heavenly scent when you bend down and smell them at close range.

In spring you have the fragrant scent of the mimosa tree, and deliciously scented freesias, hyacinths and narcissi will waft their perfume across the garden. On a warm summer night there is little to compare with the sweet perfume of jasmine and honeysuckle. Train these over a porch, a doorway, under a window or perhaps to overhang your terrace.

Datura and *Cestrum nocturnum* come to mind immediately as being delicious-smelling shrubs: find a place for each of these next to a garden seat or in a corner of your patio, where

Above *The beautiful, trumpet-shaped flowers of datura exude a rich perfume in the evening air.*

they can best be appreciated. I have also seen a datura planted in a large container on the shady side of a balcony – very striking to look at, and with the added bonus of the rich perfume emitting from the exotic, white, trumpet-shaped flowers.

The heavy scent of orange blossom at various times of the year is unmistakable, and the perfume of the solandra, similar to ripe apricots, is both attractive and unusual.

Herbs such as mint, thyme, lemon thyme, rosemary and lavender are easy to grow and will give off a strongly aromatic scent as you brush past them.

When choosing roses, whether hybrid teas or climbers, search out the most fragrant ones. Often the richer and deeper the colour, the stronger the scent. When full-scented roses are grown along with fragrant honeysuckle the effect can be quite breathtaking.

Clumps of clove carnations planted along the edges of paths will welcome visitors with their sweet smell, and trailing carnations and pinks in window boxes will fill your rooms with that unmistakable, clove-like aroma.

CONTAINER
GARDENING

4

GROWING PLANTS IN CONTAINERS

Containers make it possible to grow and enjoy a surprising variety of flowers, in places where gardening would normally be out of the question. Walls, window sills, balconies and patios can all be brightened up with container-grown plants that grow rapidly in the wonderful Spanish climate and bring the pleasures of the garden right up to your door, so to speak. In addition, containers can be used in the garden itself, either as a poolside feature or to create eye-catching focal points.

Below An attractive old clay pot looks impressive planted with alocasia macrorrhiza, or 'elephant's ears', thriving here in a sunny sheltered position.

Of course, containers do dry out rapidly in the dry season, and for this reason it may not be practical for the absentee gardener to maintain them. On the other hand, if you choose your plants wisely you can still have a lasting display of colour: cacti, succulents, geraniums, ice plants and lotus are capable of surviving for months without water.

If your property is going to be in use throughout the summer, and regular watering can be carried out, the possibilities are endless.

Most plants will need watering at least once a week in summer, far less in the winter. They will also need feeding from time to time, as their root space is restricted and valuable nutrients are used up quickly. The method of watering I use is to soak the first plant and then move on to the next, and so on. I then return to the first pot, by which time the water has been absorbed, soak it again and finish off with a gentle hose over the leaves of the plant. The best time to water is either early morning or early evening.

Containers

In Spain you will find a vast range of containers for plants, in all shapes, sizes, colours and materials. In addition you can improvise your own, making use of such items as an old wheelbarrow, a hollowed-out log, or, as many local people do in Spain, a large olive oil tin with holes punched in the base and painted a bright colour.

Choose the size of your container carefully: it must not be too large or too small for the plant or plants it will hold. If you put plants in an excessively large container, it is easy to under-water or over-water, with adverse effects on the plant. If the pot is too small or overcrowded, root growth is restricted, resulting in loss of vigour. It also causes unduly rapid drying out that adds to the problems of watering in dry weather.

I always advise buying a 'saucer' to stand

the pot on. There are two reasons for this: when you water your plants the water often runs out through the drainage hole, washing away the nutrients in the compost and dirtying the surrounding floor area. Secondly, in Spain, as I have stressed before, you cannot afford to waste precious water!

Containers come in a wide range of materials, broadly divided into those made from natural materials and those made from synthetic substances. When choosing containers, you need to consider the porosity and insulation properties of the different materials, as well as the cost.

Above *An informal pot grouping in late summer. The sculpted shapes of bamboo, yucca and cupressus sempervivens contrast effectively with brightly coloured geraniums, dianthus and dimorpotheca.*

Terracotta

In Spain you will find an amazing choice of terracotta pots, both old and new, in garden centres and 'ceramicas' (centres specializing in pottery and ceramics). All plants look 'at home' in terracotta pots, which have a pleasing texture and a mellow, red-brown, earthy colour. Due to their weight, clay pots are ideal for large or heavy plants, and will withstand high winds better than plastic pots.

Unglazed pots are porous and the compost in them may dry out quickly in hot weather. Glazed pots are more expensive, but because they are not porous, moisture loss is less of a problem. The glaze can be damaged by frost, however.

As you have probably discovered, terracotta pots of all shape and size are much cheaper to buy in Spain than in most northern European countries. There are also many attractive antique pots to choose from. Although these are more expensive, they can add character to your balcony or patio.

Plastic

Though lacking the natural charm of clay and stone, plastic containers have certain advantages. Being non-porous, they do not dry out as quickly as clay pots, and they are generally cheaper to buy. Plastic containers come in a wide range of shapes, sizes and colours, including ones that are moulded and finished to resemble stone, pottery, clay and wood. Being strong yet light, plastic containers are suitable for balconies and roof patios. However, a combination of lightweight plastic pot and soilless compost may result in plant and pot blowing over in strong winds.

Stone

Stone is another natural material that blends with most settings. It is tough, weather-resistant, and quickly acquires a patina of age that adds a mellow appearance to a patio or garden. However, natural stone is extremely heavy and therefore suitable only for permanent ground level situations. Cement-based reconstituted stone is a cheaper alternative to natural stone.

Right *Pots look more effective grouped together than in isolation. Here, geraniums, succulents and yuccas provide contrasts of colour, texture and form. All of these plants are easy to grow and will put up with infrequent watering.*

Filling and planting containers

Choosing a suitable compost can make all the difference to the success of your container-grown plants. The planting medium should crumble easily and retain moisture, while permitting free drainage and circulation of air. Experienced gardeners often make up their own compost, but ready-made composts are widely available in garden centres.

There are two types of compost for use in containers – soil-based, which consists of loam, peat, sand and fertilizers, and soilless, which is made up of peat, sand, vermiculite or perlite and fertilizers. Your local garden centre will advise on a good potting compost suitable for the Spanish climate.

Soil-based composts are heavy and ideal for large plants. They retain water well, and are easily moistened if they dry out. If your garden soil is of a reasonable texture, a mixture of half topsoil and half potting compost, mixed with a little general fertilizer, will be ideal for your containers. This mixture will retain more water than just potting compost alone.

Many plants remain in their containers for a long time, so take care to plant carefully. If the container has been used before, rinse it in mild detergent, then disinfect, and finally hose clean. The container must have drainage holes in the bottom: if it doesn't, it is quite easy to drill some. The drainage holes must not clog up with soil, so cover them with a layer of drainage material consisting of 'crocks' – pieces of broken earthenware pot or flat stones. Bridge large pieces over the drainage holes and top up with smaller crocks. Add a layer of rough gravel, about 2.5cm (1in) deep, to prevent compost from washing down into the crocks.

Place a layer of compost in the bottom of the container. Carefully remove the plant from its nursery container and place it centrally in its new container, taking care not to disturb the rootball. Trickle compost between the rootball and the sides of the container, firming it gently with your fingers as you go. Thoroughly water in to help settle the compost around the roots. The compost should reach 4–6cm (2–3in) below the rim of the pot, to allow for watering.

Right *Bougainvilleas need very little attention and will grow in almost any sunny spot. This one is planted in a large concrete container – in time it will provide a splash of bright colour against the natural stone wall.*

WINDOW BOXES

Window boxes bursting with gaily coloured flowers add character to any house or apartment, and will give pleasure to passers-by as well as to the owners. Seville is a city renowned for its window box displays. Do try and visit in May or June; the flowers at this time of the year are quite breathtaking and will give you plenty of inspiration.

To ensure that the box retains enough moisture to support the plants, it should be at least 25cm (10in) deep, and to ensure good drainage it should be raised slightly above the window-sill. Place a drip tray underneath the box, to protect passers-by if you happen to be a little heavy-handed with the watering.

The easiest and most prolific-growing plants for window boxes are cacti, geraniums, dianthus (pinks) and ice plants. Trailing plants such as geraniums and hanging carnations will spill over the container and add to the exuberant effect. All of these plants flower pro-

Above *Window boxes brimming over with trailing geraniums in a single colour look very striking.*

fusely, but when they become untidy and leggy they are best replaced with new plants or cuttings. They withstand extremes of temperature and are undemanding, yet create a spectacular show throughout the year.

If you are staying in Spain throughout the summer months and can water your window boxes regularly, you might consider growing begonias, bijou sweet peas and nasturtiums.

When choosing plants, select colours and shapes to create an eye-catching display. Avoid tall plants which are vulnerable to wind, but aim for a variety of plant height and growth habit: a row of plants all of the same height looks uniform and uninteresting. Think about foliage, too: some geraniums have attractive, variegated leaves, and the blue-grey, fleshy leaves of ice plants create contrast.

PATIOS

In northern Europe we tend to think of a patio as a sun terrace or a quiet, paved area of the garden. However, in Spain a patio is really an enclosed courtyard, an area of tranquility where you can take a cool drink or a meal with your family and friends, shaded from the unrelenting sun in the summer months. Most gardens have a special area for sitting out, and container-grown plants can be positioned here to bring colour and scent right to the place where they can be most appreciated. An attractive grouping of pots and plants can soften and break up the expanse of a paved area, create points of emphasis, and give a feeling of intimacy.

Try not to overcrowd the patio area; quiet understatement is better suited to an area that is primarily for relaxation. A few pots strategically placed, a climber or two, and perhaps a centre piece such as a fountain, a statue or an ornamental pot, are all you need to create a cool and pleasant refuge in which to sit and pass the time of day.

Even for the absentee gardener, the choice of plants for growing in containers is wide. Group pots of clivia, amaryllis or cineraria to bloom in time for Easter, agapanthus and cannas to bloom in summer, and for all-year round interest, the ever-versatile geraniums, cacti and succulents. For shady areas, choose asparagus ferns, cheese plants, hostas and Arum lilies.

Citrus trees look very attractive growing in containers. Because the roots are restricted, the trees tend to be smaller but they produce excellent fruit. They do need regular watering and feeding, however, and so for the absentee gardener are not always ideal unless you have someone to help with the watering. The trees can be moved indoors for the winter: place in a sunny position and watch out for any pests on the leaves. When you bring the plant outdoors again in the spring, do not move it into bright sunshine straight away, as sudden changes in temperature can damage new growth.

Below *A pool and fountain form a central feature in this courtyard and create a 'cool' atmosphere.*

Right *A spectacular deciduous climber, bignonia rosa will grow well in a large, deep container if there is no soil at the base of the wall.*

Tall foliage plants will add height and shape to a patio grouping. Palms and yuccas are excellent in this context, and require very little watering. Oleanders, bamboo and bay trees are also suited to pot growth. Plant them individually or in large pots, surrounded by geraniums and ice plants. Different plants can be combined in pots as long as they all have the same water needs.

Bougainvillea, bignonia, plumbago, wisteria, jasmine and honeysuckle are just some of the climbing plants that can be trained against the walls around your patio, masking the brickwork and creating a pleasant sense of enclosure. If they can't be planted in the earth, choose a large, deep pot that will accommodate the roots. If it has a narrow neck, all the better, as it will not dry out so quickly in hot weather.

In addition to your plants, you can hang beautiful ceramic tiles or plates on the walls surrounding your patio. Garden ornaments or large antique pots positioned amongst your plants and garden furniture will add further interest.

BALCONIES

On balconies, plants can be grown in large planters of lightweight material such as fibreglass or plastic. Always check how much weight your balcony can hold: large pots become very heavy when filled with soil.

Arrange sun-loving plants at the outer edge of the balcony where there is more light, and shade-lovers towards the back. Window boxes can be positioned on top of the balcony walls, but they must be safely secured with brackets.

On balconies, it is important to bear in mind that plants in containers can be damaged by hot, dry summer winds and cold winter winds, not to mention the unrelenting sun.

If you have little shelter from the elements, or if you are away for much of the time and cannot water your plants regularly, you can plant cacti and succulents, which need little or no attention. You can if you wish plant geraniums or dianthus in between the cacti for added colour. Another useful plant that needs very little attention is *Lotus berthelotii*. It withstands months of dry weather, thriving in full sun and dry soil.

If you are able to water more regularly, there are plenty of plants to choose from, such as gloxinias, bijou sweet peas, petunias and begonias. Nasturtiums are particularly fond of sun and dry conditions, as are herbs such as rosemary and lavender.

HANGING BASKETS

Wall-mounted or hanging baskets, imaginatively planted, will brighten up an expanse of wall or ceiling on a balcony or patio. However, unless you are staying at your holiday home for some months, or are a permanent resident, I would not recommend hanging baskets as they dry out so rapidly and therefore need frequent watering.

Hanging baskets are usually made from galvanized or plastic-coated wire. Another type is the solid basket, available in terracotta or plastic and often provided with a built-in drip tray. Some versions have a built-in water reservoir inside, which is very valuable when watering is infrequent.

It goes without saying that hanging baskets should be attached to the wall or ceiling using brackets that are strong enough to carry their weight when filled with wet potting mix and plants. Try also to position them in a spot that is sheltered from winds.

What to plant

The absentee gardener would be wise to choose plants that will not suffer too badly if watering cannot be done every day. Cacti and succulents are ideal, as they have their own built-in water supply, and plants such as geraniums and dianthus are also drought-tolerant. If you are able to water more frequently, then your choice of plants is much wider: fuchsias, asparagus grass, lobelia, nasturtiums, impatiens and French marigolds are all suitable for hanging baskets. Remember that the basket should look attractive when seen from below as well as from all sides: trailing geraniums, lobelia and fuchsias will create a 'ball' of colour that disguises the basket itself.

Filling and planting

The most convenient way to fill a wire hanging

Left On balconies, most plants should be arranged at the outer edge where there is more light.

basket is to rest it on a large pot or bucket. Line the inside of the basket with plastic sheeting and pierce a few drainage holes in the bottom of the lining. Put a trowel full of charcoal in the bottom of the basket to aid drainage and keep the compost 'sweet', then fill the basket almost to the top with a good soil and compost mix. Leave a watering space at the top of about 2.5cm (1in). Water well.

Using a sharp knife, cut slits in the plastic lining around the sides of the basket and push the roots of trailing plants between the wires, from the outside into the potting mix, embedding them firmly. These trailing plants will cascade downwards as they grow, lending a softening effect to the arrangement.

Now plant the top of the basket. Set the tallest plants in the centre and trailing and edging plants around them. Firm more planting mix in around the plants, then water in gently.

Watering and feeding

Because they are so small, hanging baskets dry out rapidly and require watering every day, particularly during the hottest months. Always water in the early morning or in the evening. A weekly feed with a compound liquid fertilizer is also essential, since the frequency of watering washes many of the nutrients out of the compost before they have been absorbed by the roots.

Try to position your hanging basket in a place where it can conveniently be reached for watering and general maintenance. You may have to use a step ladder to reach containers placed high up on a wall or ceiling. A useful tip for watering these containers is to use an improvised hose extension: a long cane or stick tied to the end section of the hosepipe will keep the pipe rigid, enabling you to water the basket from ground level. Make sure the basket will drip where it doesn't matter, or use pots with built-in drip trays.

PLANT PROBLEMS

In the four years that we have had our villa in Spain, we have had very few problems with pests and diseases in the garden – perhaps we have just been lucky! Generally, plant pests and diseases are less of a problem in Spain than they are in northern Europe, where the warm, damp springs and summers encourage all kinds of nasties to breed and develop. However, even the most carefully looked after garden in Spain will have its share of problems from time to time; some years will be better than others, depending on the vagaries of the weather.

Preventing problems
Prevention is better than cure, and a lot of wasted effort can be avoided if you take swift, precautionary measures against plant pests and diseases as soon as they are spotted. It is often possible to avoid the time, trouble and expense of using hazardous and environmentally-suspect pesticides by following these common-sense rules:

First, give your plants the best possible growing conditions. The soil should be well drained and aerated and contain enough moisture and nutrients to ensure that plants grow strong and healthy and thus have a greater chance of resisting attack by pests and diseases. Weak, slow-growing plants succumb to attack more readily. Strong growth is encouraged by applying a dressing of compost or well-rotted manure around the base of your plants during autumn and winter and a good dressing of general fertilizer during the spring.

Weeds on paths and driveways can be cleared by applying a path weedkiller. The weeds usually take two or three weeks to clear, and stronger weeds such as thistles may need a further application.

Lawn weedkillers should be applied in the spring and not in the summer, when the intense heat of the sun may turn your lawn brown.

The same procedure applies to pots and containers. It is a good idea to remove the top 5cm (2in) of old compost every so often and replace with a dressing of fresh compost and fertilizer.

Always practise good garden hygiene. Prunings, for example, should always be burned – never leave them lying about under trees and bushes. Similarly, garden rubbish and pieces of wood left lying around will encourage snails to make their homes there. Remove weeds regularly, as they supply cover for insects and are centres of infection.

Make sure that the plants you buy from garden centres and markets are healthy and sturdy, and choose disease-resistant strains whenever possible.

Dealing with weeds
We have found very little weed growth in our garden in Spain. Presumably this is due once again to the dryness of the climate. Lack of rainfall does have some benefits!

Shallow-rooted annual weeds growing between shrubs and flowers are best cleared by working the soil with a hoe and removing by hand. Mulching around the plants will smother the weeds by depriving them of light and water.

Perennial weeds are more of a problem as they often grow strong tap roots that are difficult to remove. If you are unable to dig out the roots of dock leaves or fennel you may have to resort to chemical methods of getting rid of them. Cut out as much of the root as possible, then use a knife to split the root that remains in the soil and apply a small amount of undiluted weedkiller to kill off the root and prevent the weed growing again.

Aphids
The most common pests you will find in your garden in Spain are aphids – in other words, greenfly, blackfly and whitefly. These are usually found feeding under leaves, on new

shoots and around leaf and flower buds. The tell-tale signs of aphids are curling leaves and a sticky, honeydew secretion on young buds. Aphids feed on the tissue of new young shoots and cause leaf malformation that spoils the appearance of plants as well as affecting fresh growth and the formation of flowers.

These little thugs thrive particularly well on plants that are short of water, so make sure, where possible, that your plants are watered and fed properly. Minor infestations can be dealt with by squashing the insects with finger and thumb. Cut off any badly infected shoots and burn them. In bad cases, spray with a systemic insecticide on a calm, windless day, in either the early morning or early evening. Remember to spray the undersides of the leaves as well as the tops.

For the absentee gardener, 'when to spray' is often difficult to time. If you can spray young shoots, leaves and tips in the spring, perhaps during the Easter holidays, this will give you a head start in the fight against aphids. If you can then follow with another spray in May or June, you will probably manage to keep these pests well under control.

Snails and caterpillars
A tell-tale sign that you have a snail or cater-pillar problem is the appearance of holes in the leaves of your plant. Dust periodically around your plants with a snail and caterpillar dust.

Fungal diseases
Powdery mildew, rust and leaf spot are plant diseases caused by fungi. These generally affect herbaceous and woody plants such as roses, but can also affect fruit trees, geraniums and ice plants. Tell-tale signs are leaves covered in white, powdery patches or reddish-brown spots. Growth slows down and flower buds fail to open. Spray affected plants with a fungicide in the spring and again in early summer, or when affected. Combined fungicides and systemic insecticides are available, the advantage of these is that they will tackle aphids and fungal disease simultaneously.

Above *Keeping the soil clear of weeds encourages healthy plants and discourages pests.*

Fungal disease usually affects plants grown in crowded or enclosed situations. If necessary, thin the plants to ensure a good flow of air around them.

Mineral deficiencies
There are two common mineral deficiencies associated with the calcareous soils often found in Spain. One is a shortage of nitrogen and the other is a shortage of iron.

When young leaves are generally of a yellow hue, the oldest leaves are mostly yellow and the lower leaves have a tendency to drop, this is probably a sign of nitrogen deficiency. This can be corrected by using a good fertilizer, preferably one that provides mainly nitrogen. (Similar symptoms arise in plants that are not receiving enough light; if this is the case, reduce shade by cutting back any nearby overhanging branches or move the affected plants to a new position.)

When new leaves appear yellow and upper leaves turn yellow while the veins remain green, this is a sign that your plants are lacking iron. You can buy iron pellets from a garden centre: scatter the recommended amount around the base of the affected plants, add a good handful of compost, and water in well.

USEFUL ENGLISH/SPANISH TERMS

Acacia	Mimosa	Dahlia	Dalia
Agapanthus	Agapante	Daisy	Margarita
Agave	Pita, agave	Datura	Estramonio, dativía
Almond	Almendro	Deciduous	Hoja caduca
Aloe	Aloe	Dianthus	Clavellina
Amaryllis	Amarilis	Dig, to	Cavar, excavar
Anemone	Anémone	Disease	Enfermedad
Annual	Anual	Drought	Sequia
Antirrhinum	Antirrino	Dust	Polvo
Apricot	Albaricoque		
Arum lily	Cala	Earth	Tierra
Asparagus fern	Esparraguera	Eucalyptus	Eucalipto
Aster	Aster	Evergreen	Arbol de hoja perenne
Autumn	Otoño		
Avocado	Aguacete	Fertilizer	Abono
Axe	Hacha, segur	Fig tree	Higuera
		Flower	Flor
Balcony	Balcón	Flower bed	Macizo
Basket	Cesta	Flower bud	Capullo
Bay	Laurel	Flower pot	Maceta
Bee	Abeja	Fly	Mosca
Begonia	Begonia	Fork	Horca
Biennial	Bienal	Fragrant	Fragante
Bignonia	Bignonia	Freesia	Fresia
Black	Negro	Frost	Helada
Black fly	Mosca negra	Fruit	Fruta
Blackspot	Mancha negra	Fuchsia	Fucsia
Blue	Azul	Fungicide	Fungicida
Bougainvillea	Buganvilla		
Broom (shrub)	Hiniesta	Garden centre	Vivero
Broom	Escoba	Garlic	Ajo
Brown	Moreno	Gazania	Gazania
Bucket	Cubo	Geranium	Geranio
Busy Lizzie	Impatiens de jardín	Gladiolus	Gladiolo
		Gloxinia	Gloxiena
Cactus	Cacto	Godetia	Godecia
Canna	Caña de Indias	Grapefruit	Pomelo
Carnation	Clavel	Grass	Hierba
Carob	Algarrobo	Gravel	Grava
Carpobrutus	Uña de León	Green	Verde
Ceonothus	Chaquira	Green fly	Pulga
Cestrum nocturnum	Galén de noche		
Chrysanthemum	Crisantemo	Hammer	Martillo
Clementine	Clementina	Hedge	Seto
Climber	Trepador	Hedgecutter (electric)	Tijera eléctrica
Clivia	Clivia	Helichrysum	Siempreviva
Colour	Color	Herb	Hierba
Compound fertilizer	Abono compuesto	Hibiscus	Hibisco, pacifico
Crocus	Azafrán	Hoe	Escardillo
Cupressus	Ciprés	Honeysuckle	Madreselva
Cyclamen	Ciclamino	Hosepipe	Manguera
		Humidity	Humedad
Daffodil	Narciso	Hyacinth	Jacinto

English	Spanish	English	Spanish
Ice plants	Flor de Cucaillo	Path	Senda
Impatiens	Impatiens de Jardín	Peat	Turba
Insecticide	Insecticida	Perennial	Hoja perenne
Ipomors	Campanilla	Pest	Plaga
Iris	Lirio de jardín	Petunia	Petunia
Ivy	Hiedra	Phlox	Flox
		Phosphate	Fosfato
Jacaranda	Jacaranda	Pick-axe	Pico
Jasmine	Jazmín	Pine	Pino
		Pink (dianthus)	Clavellina
Lantana	Lantana, bandera española	Pink (colour)	Rosa
		Plant root	Raíz
Lavender	Lavendula, espliego	Plumbago	Plumbago, jasmín azúl
Lawn	Césped	Poinsettia	Flor de Pascua
Lawn-mower (electric)	Cortacésped eléctrico	Pomegranate	Granado
Lawn-mower (hand)	Cortacésped manual	Poppy	Amapola
Lawn-mower (motor)	Cortacésped motor a gasolina	Portulaca	Verdolaga
		Purple	Purpureo, morado
Lawn-mower (rotary)	Cortacésped rotativo	Pyracantha	Espino de Fuego
Leaf	Hoja		
Lemon tree	Limonero		
Lily	Lirio, Azucena	Rain	Lluvia
Lime	Cal	Rake	Rastrillo
Liquid fertilizer	Fertilizante concentrado líquido	Red	Rojo
		Ripe	Maduro
Livingstone Daisy	Margarita de Livingstone	Rose	Rosa
		Rosemary (shrub, herb)	Romero
Long-arm pruners	Cortarramas de cuerda	Rubber tree	Arbol del caucho
Loquat	Níspero	Ruschia	Mesem
Manure	Estiércol		
Marigold	Caléndula	Sage	Salvia
Marjoram	Mejorana	Salvia	Salvia
Mattock/Spanish hoe	Azada, azadón, escardillo, azadilla	Sand	Arena
		Schinus	Falso pimiento
Mint	Hierba buena, menta	Screw	Tornillo
Morning glory	Campanilla	Screwdriver	Destornillador
Mow, to	Segar	Secateurs	Tijeras para podar
Myporem	Transparente	Seed	Semilla
		Shade	Sombra
Nail	Clavo	Shrub	Arbusto
Narcissus	Narciso	Sieve	Criba
Nasturtium	Capuchina	Snail	Caracol
Nitrate	Nitrato	Solandra	Solandra
		Solanum	Solanum
Oleander	Adelfa	Spade, shovel	Pala
Olive	Oliva	Spiraea	Espirea
Orange	Naranjo	Sprinkler	Rociadera
Orange tree	Naranjo	Spring	Primavera
Orchard	Huerto	Stake	Estaca
Overcast	Nubloso	Statice	Acelga silvestre
		Step ladder	Escalera
Palm	Palmera	Stick	Palo
Pampas grass	Hierba de las Pampas	Stock	Alhelí
Parsley	Perejíl	Stone	Piedra
Patio	Patio	String	Pita, cuerda

Summer	Verano	Water	Agua
Sun	Sol	Water, to	Regar
Sunflower	Girasol		
Sweet pea	Guisante de olor	Watering can	Regadera
		Wheelbarrow	Carretilla
		White	Blanco
Tamarisk	Tamarisco, tamarix	Window box	Jardinera de ventana
Tarragon	Estragón	Winter	Invierno
Thin out, to	Entresacar	Wisteria	Wistaria
Thunbergia	Ojo de poeta		
Thyme	Tomillo	Yellow	Amarillo
Transplant, to	Transplantar	Yucca	Yuca
Tree bark	Corteza		
Tree branch	Rama		
Tree trunk	Tronco	Zantedeschia	Cala
Tree	Arbol	Zinnia	Zinnia
Tulip	Tulipán		
Vegetable	Legumbre		
Verbena	Verbena		

GARDENS TO VISIT

Barcelona
Jardín Botánico de Barcelona,
Avenida Muntayno, Montjuic

Blanes
Jardín de Aclimatación,
Pinya de Rosa

Jardín Botánico Marimurtra (Mar y Murtra),
Fundación Carlos Faust

Canary Islands
Jardín de Botánico Viera y Clavijo
Tafira Alta
and
Parque Doramas
Las Palmas de Gran Canárias

Jardín de Aclimatación de la Orotava,
Puerto de la Cruz, Tenerife

Cordoba
The gardens and courtyards of the Viana
Palace Museum

The gardens of the Alcázar
Window boxes and patios in the
Barrio de la Judería

Elche
The Palm Forest, Huerto del Curo

Granada
The gardens of the Generalife

Mallorca
Son Alfabia – country residence with Arab
gardens, sub-tropical vegetation and water

Seville
The gardens of the Alcázar
Jardines de la Delicias, Paseo de las Delicias
Jardines de Christina, Avenida de Roma
Jardines de Murillo, Plaza de Santa Cruz
Parque de Maria de Luisa, Plaza de Espana
Window boxes throughout the city

Valencia
Jardín de Botánico, Calle Cuarte

GLOSSARY

Annual A plant that grows from seed and completes its life cycle in a year or less, either from spring to autumn or autumn to late summer.

Biennial A plant that requires two growing seasons to complete its life cycle. The seed germinates and grows during the first year, and flowers, seeds and dies in the following year.

Bract Colourful modified leaves surrounding the true, often insignificant flowers of some plants (e.g. poinsettia, bougainvillea).

Bulb An underground stem that stores food reserves in many overlapping fleshy scales. The centre of the bulb contains the bulb shoot and the roots grow from the base. The bulb is usually enclosed in a thin papery covering.

Bulbous plants All plants that have underground storage systems for food and moisture are termed bulbous plants.

Calcareous soil A type of soil that contains calcium carbonate, which is only slightly soluble in water. This material is particularly difficult when it forms an impenetrable layer, known as caliche, which can often be up to 20m (6ft) thick. Plant roots are unable to grow through the thick layers of calcium.

Corm A swollen, rounded, underground stem used by some plants for food storage. It is flat at the top and the roots grow from the base. During the growing season it produces clumps of new cormlets at the side which can be broken off at the end of the growing season and will produce new flowers for the following year.

Crown The junction between the root and the stem of a plant, at or near ground level.

Deciduous Plants, particularly trees and shrubs, that lose their leaves each year, usually in winter, and grow fresh new leaves in the following spring.

Dead-head To remove faded or dead flower heads to prevent the plant wasting its energy on seed formation, thus prolonging the flowering season.

Evergreen A tree or shrub that retains its leaves all year.

Mulch A layer of material spread on the soil around plants to conserve moisture, check weed growth, supply nutrients, or all three of these. Organic mulches include bark clippings, wood chips, leaf mould, grass clippings, compost or manure. Inorganic mulches include gravel, granite, rock or plastic. Inorganic mulches are a cheap, low-maintenance way of covering large areas.

Perennial A plant that grows, flowers and multiplies year after year.

Pinching out Removal of the growing tip of a stem to encourage the growth of flower buds or to produce new branches.

Pruning The cutting back of branches or shoots of plants, shrubs or trees, to restrict size, improve shape or promote growth of flowers, fruit or buds.

Rhizome A thick underground stem which grows at or just below ground level. Rhizomes usually grow horizontally and produce shoots at their tips which are sent above ground, e.g. iris. Pieces that break off a rhizome will root and produce new plants.

Succulent Any plant which stores water in fleshy stems and/or leaves.

Systemic Pesticide that is absorbed internally, working through the sap of plants.

Top-dressing The addition of a layer of compost, manure or fertilizer to the surface of the soil around plants to maintain fertility.

Tuber A thickened fleshy underground storage organ, either stem or root, which swells with plant food as it grows. The most common flower growing from a tuber is the dahlia.

Variegated A term applied to leaves or petals that are patterned or blotched with contrasting hues.

PLANT INDEX